Winter Games Made Simple

Winter Games Made Simple

A guide for spectators & television viewers

DAN BARTGES

Turner Publishing, Inc.
ATLANTA

COPYRIGHT ©1993 BY DAN BARTGES. ALL RIGHTS RESERVED.
NO PART OF THE CONTENTS OF THIS BOOK MAY BE REPRODUCED OR UTILIZED
IN ANY FORM OR BY ANY MEANS, ELECTRONIC OR MECHANICAL, INCLUDING
PHOTOCOPYING, RECORDING, OR BY ANY INFORMATION STORAGE AND RETRIEVAL
SYSTEM, WITHOUT THE WRITTEN CONSENT OF THE PUBLISHER.

PUBLISHED BY TURNER PUBLISHING, INC.
A SUBSIDIARY OF TURNER BROADCASTING SYSTEM, INC.
1050 TECHWOOD DRIVE, N.W.
ATLANTA, GEORGIA 30318

FIRST EDITION 10 9 8 7 6 5 4 3 2 1

Library of Congress Cataloging-in-Publication Data

Bartges, Dan, 1948–
    Winter games made simple : a guide for spectators & television viewers / Dan Bartges.
      p.   cm.
    Includes bibliographical references (p. 106) and Index.
    ISBN 1-878685-56-2
    1. Winter Olympics. I. Title
GV841.5.B37   1993
796.98—dc20   93–32015
                                                                                                                                                        CIP

DISTRIBUTED BY ANDREWS AND MCMEEL
A UNIVERSAL PRESS SYNDICATE COMPANY
4900 MAIN STREET
KANSAS CITY, MISSOURI 64112

EDITORIAL:

VICE PRESIDENT, EDITORAL—WALTON RAWLS
EDITOR—CRAWFORD BARNETT
COPY EDITOR—MARIAN LORD

DESIGN:

VICE PRESIDENT, DESIGN AND PRODUCTION—MICHAEL J. WALSH
ILLUSTRATIONS—DAVID JACKSON
PHOTO RESEARCH—MARTY MOORE
PRODUCTION COORDINATOR—ANNE MURDOCH

FILM PREPARATION BY GRAPHICS INTERNATIONAL,
ATLANTA, GEORGIA.
PRINTED AND BOUND BY R. R. DONNELLEY, CRAWFORDSVILLE, INDIANA

PRINTED IN THE U.S.A.

Contents

INTRODUCTION • 6 »

BIATHLON • 12 »

BOBSLED • 20 »

FIGURE SKATING • 30 »

ICE HOCKEY • 50 »

LUGE • 62 »

SKIING • 70 »

SPEEDSKATING • 98 »

BIBLIOGRAPHY • 106 »

INDEX • 108 »

Welcome to the Winter Olympics

In 1875, German archaeologists made a remarkable discovery on the ancient battlefields of southern Greece: they uncovered the site of the original Olympic Games, thereby sparking a renewed interest in the greatest tradition in sports history, a tradition that dates back twenty-seven hundred years to Olympia, Greece.

First recorded in 776 B.C., the ancient Olympics were religious celebrations honoring Zeus, the ruling god of the Greek pantheon, and centered upon just one sporting event, a foot race of about two hundred yards. A young cook named Coroebus of Elis won that first race, for which he was awarded high praise, prestige, and an olive wreath.

More contests were added over time, such as wrestling, the discus throw, boxing, and chariot racing. For more than a thousand years the ancient Olympics continued, taking place every four years, until A.D. 393 when the Roman emperor Theodosius banned the Games, probably, according to his-

The Olympic logo of five interlocking circles symbolizes the bonds of friendship among the five major continents. It was first used on the official Olympic flag in 1920.

torians, because he disliked their pagan origins.

Fifteen hundred years passed before the Olympic flame was rekindled, ignited through the tireless efforts of a young, idealistic French baron named Pierre de Coubertin. Coubertin hoped the renewed Games would foster goodwill among nations, and in 1896 athletes from thirteen countries gathered to compete in Athens, Greece. The high-point of the first modern Games was the marathon, which was won by a twenty-six-year-old Greek shepherd named Spiridon Louis, who ran the historic distance from Marathon to Athens.

By 1920 there was growing sentiment—particularly among countries where climate made skiing and ice skating popular—to create a venue for cold-weather sports. In response to this demand, a group, once again spearheaded by the indefatigable Baron de Coubertin, organized a winter competition. Making its debut in January 1924, that first Winter Olympics, in Chamonix, France, attracted nearly three hundred athletes from sixteen nations and included ice hockey, figure skating, speedskating, cross-country skiing, and ski jumping. (The first Alpine skiing contests, such as the downhill and slalom, were not introduced into Olympic competition until 1936.) As might have been expected, athletes from snowy northern Europe dominated, particularly those from Norway and Finland.

Having grown greatly since their inception, recent Games have drawn about eighteen hundred athletes from more than sixty countries. These athletes—the finest in the world—assemble to test their skills, forge lasting friendships, and perpetuate the Games' founding spirit of international goodwill and sportsmanship.

Due to its array of captivating events, diversity of competitors, and global television exposure, the Winter Olympics has become one of the most popular sporting events in the world. Like the Summer Olympics, the Winter Olympics is held every four years. From 1924 through 1992 (except when suspended in 1940 and 1944 during World War II), both the Summer and Winter Games were held during the same year. The events are now separated by two years. For example: the 1994 Winter Olympics in Lillehammer, Norway, and the 1996 Summer Olympics in Atlanta, Georgia.

In addition to providing spectators with the adrenaline-charged drama and excitement of split-second finishes and dazzling athletic feats, the Olympic Games offer inspiring insight into the extent of human potential and emotional strength. There is obvious motivation among all athletes to win their events, but their relentless drive is also fueled by the desire for personal perfection. After all, less than 15 percent of the contestants take home an Olympic medal.

This value placed on personal achievement can be seen in the actions of

The high level of competition at the Olympics inspires many athletes to give the performances of their lives.

American figure skater Brian Boitano. Following his performance in the tense finals of the 1988 Olympics, Boitano did not even watch to see if arch rival Brian Orser could outpoint him. While Orser skated before a worldwide audience, Boitano was in the locker room, happily wiping his skate blades and listening to his Walkman. He felt that he had accomplished what he had set years before as his goal: He had finally skated to the best of his ability. (Incidentally, Boitano won the gold medal.)

Similarly, after Alpine skiing legend Ingemar Stenmark captured two gold medals in the 1980 Winter Games at Lake Placid, the reticent Swede remarked, "History is not important. The important thing is that I am satisfied with myself."

Each Winter Olympics is enhanced by impressive stories of dogged persistence, fortitude, and courage. Olympic great Scott Hamilton overcame childhood illness and a frail physique to earn the gold medal in figure skating (1984). When asked about his secret to overcoming the intense stress of self-doubt and competitive pressures, the good-natured Hamilton responded, "I hold my breath all day and then go back to my room to breathe."

When Christl Haas was just three years old, she informed her parents that she intended to become a top ski racer; when she was twenty, the determined Austrian won the gold medal in the downhill (1964). It is said that Dick Button's first coach told him he would never succeed as an Olympian. Fortunately, Button believed in himself more than the words of others. After switching coaches he went on to dominate the sport of figure skating, capturing two Olympic gold medals along the way in 1948 and 1952.

Olympic success is also about willpower and testing the limits of one's skill and control. Despite the inherent dangers of many Olympic events, such as the luge and the downhill, the steps to the top of the awards platform are rarely climbed by athletes who consider themselves to be daredevils. Every nuance of an event has been rehearsed until it becomes second nature for the participant and much of the risk has been removed. Even ski jumpers, who soar down the side of a mountain at 55 mph, would argue that their sport is fundamentally about mental toughness and risk management, not about recklessness.

Given that all Olympic contenders are accomplished athletes who have mastered the technical aspects of their respective sports, the one ingredient that seems to elevate the few to the gold-medal level is the ability to maintain intense concentration. In each Olympic sport, the athletes know that the slightest flicker in concentration could cost them a medal.

All training regimens, therefore, focus on mastering concentration skills as well as physical skills. Champion speedskaters who have focused intensely during a race talk afterwards of feeling as though they had skated in slow motion, which made it much easier for them to maintain precise timing and technique for a superior effort. Likewise, many ski jumpers who have attained deep concentration could swear after a great jump that they had glided for several minutes rather than only a few seconds. And champion fig-

In the opening ceremony of each Olympics, athletes parade into the main stadium. Countries enter in alphabetical order except for Greece, which always leads the procession, and the host country, which concludes the parade.

ure skaters, after near-perfect performances, can often recall a rich sense of joy and freedom but very little of the actual performances. These deep levels of concentration, during which intuitive action seems to predominate, are almost trancelike for many top athletes, who speak of being "in the zone" while they compete.

With continuing advances in sports science, virtually all modern Olympic athletes are so highly trained that even the smallest edge can translate into victory. This rarified level of competition coupled with the high-stakes commercialization of the Olympic Games often spawns a crowd of specialists who supervise and travel with the athletes. These include not only coaches and trainers, but physiotherapists, sports psychologists, public relations people, financial advisors, and nutritionists. For better and for worse, the Olympics has become big business.

The complexity of the Winter Games is nowhere more evident than in the space-age technology that delivers the exciting events to millions of televi-

The flame that burns throughout the Winter Games is a ceremonial link between the ancient and modern Olympics. In early Greece a flame burned at the sacred altar of Zeus during Olympic festivities.

sion viewers worldwide. For example, remote-controlled minicams the size of a lipstick case are sometimes mounted on a bobsled or a skier's helmet for a thrilling, televised vantage point that until recently only the athletes themselves could experience.

In the more remote locales, robotic cameras with zoom lenses, pan/tilt devices, and cold-weather housing are used to increase the viewers' access. Video transmission is made through advanced fiberoptic cable, microwave, or satellite, from the event venues to the TV network's Olympic broadcast center. From there, the video signal is relayed to satellite uplink stations, on to receiving stations, and then shot back up for satellite transmission throughout America. All this is achieved within seconds.

Despite the magnitude and complexity of the modern Winter Olympics, however, there's little doubt that fast-running Coroebus of Elis would approve. He would still recognize that enduring spirit and excitement which existed when, watching from the heavens, Zeus himself was a spectator.

SITES OF THE WINTER OLYMPICS

1924	Chamonix, France
1928	St. Moritz, Switzerland
1932	Lake Placid, United States
1936	Garmisch-Partenkirchen, Germany
1940 & 1944	Games suspended due to World War II
1948	St. Moritz, Switzerland
1952	Oslo, Norway
1956	Cortina d'Ampezzo, Italy
1960	Squaw Valley, United States
1964	Innsbruck, Austria
1968	Grenoble, France
1972	Sapporo, Japan
1976	Innsbruck, Austria
1980	Lake Placid, United States
1984	Sarajevo, Yugoslavia
1988	Calgary, Canada
1992	Albertville, France
1994	Lillehammer, Norway
1998	Nagano, Japan

BIATHLON • 12

Biathlon

An obscure sport to most Americans, the biathlon is one of the Winter Olympics' most demanding events. It requires the mastery of two contrary skills: the all-out physical effort of cross-country skiing and the calm, controlled steadiness of expert marksmanship. In a biathlon, competitors ski a grueling cross-country course, stop at a shooting range to fire their rifles at coin-sized targets, and immediately resume skiing at racing pace.

In a biathlon race, the athletes—each shouldering a rifle—depart the starting line at one-minute intervals to ski a cross-country trail, or "course," that begins and ends in a stadium and spectator area. The stadium area also features the penalty track and shooting range.

Although there are several biathlon events, each with its own requirements, all involve cross-country skiing and tests of marksmanship. In the men's 10-kilometer (6.2-mile) race, for example, the competitors ski cross-country for 2.5 kilometers, then stop at the firing range to shoot at five targets with only five bullets, resume skiing for 5 kilometers, stop to shoot five more targets, then press on for 2.5 more kilometers and the finish line. The first shooting sequence is from the prone position, the second is standing.

The other men's events are the individual 20K, which has four shooting sequences, and the 4 x 7.5K relay, where each member of a four-man relay team skis three 2.5K loops and shoots two sequences before tagging his teammate. In the relay, the biathlete is allowed eight bullets per sequence to hit five targets instead of the usual five bullets. Also, all teams start at the same time in the relay event instead of at one-minute intervals.

> The official motto of the Olympics is "Swifter, Higher, Stronger." Taken from the Latin *Citius, Altius, Fortius*—literally "Faster, Higher, Braver"—it was first used in 1895 by Father Henri Didon, a French educator.

In the women's biathlon, the events are the 7.5K with two shooting sequences, the 15K with four shooting sequences, and a 3 x 7.5K relay (three women on each team). With the exception of different skiing distances, the women's races are identical to the men's.

In all events, the best time wins, but marksmanship can influence time heavily. For every missed target in the men's 20K and women's 15K events—referred to as the "individual" events—a one-minute penalty is added to the overall time. In the other events—called "sprints"—each missed target requires one "penalty loop" around a 150-meter (492-foot) track, which adds costly time.

COMPETITORS

As the biathlete approaches the firing range after completing a long stretch of cross-country skiing, the immediate challenge is to calm down in order to shoot the targets. On the arduous cross-country course, the athlete's heart rate has accelerated to about 180 beats per minute and breathing is labored. Upon reaching the rifle range, the racer must stop, gain complete composure, aim the rifle with unwavering accuracy, and shoot five small targets. This significant mind-over-body feat challenges even these athletes who have the stamina of champion marathon runners.

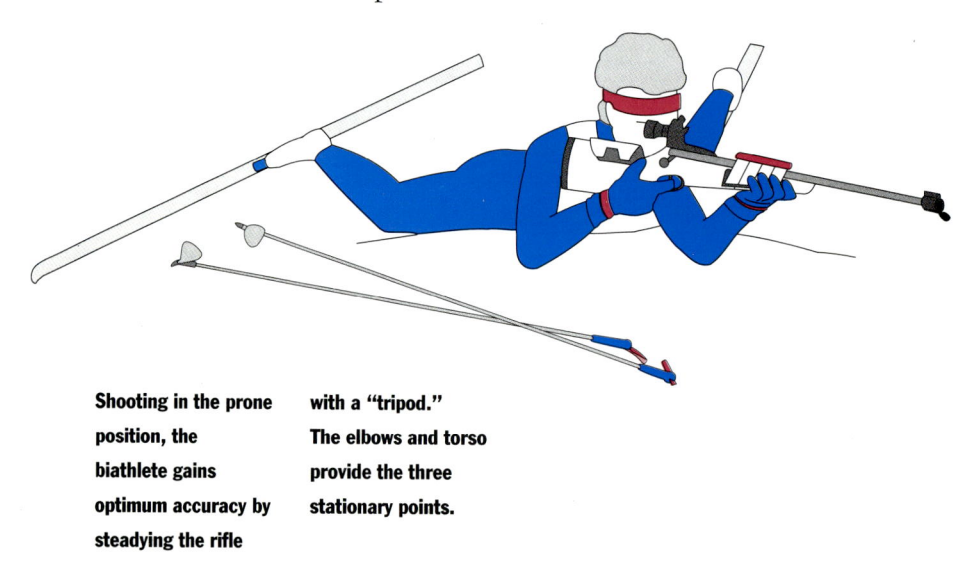

Shooting in the prone position, the biathlete gains optimum accuracy by steadying the rifle with a "tripod." The elbows and torso provide the three stationary points.

Unlike most competitors, the biathlete does not want to maintain a continuous state of excitement and tension but must be able to assume an almost stoic composure at the firing line in order to shoot accurately. Because marksmanship requires calm, precise movement and intense concentration, the biathlete needs to avoid as much adrenaline flow as possible.

How is this accomplished? Physical conditioning, combined with great technical ability in shooting and cross-country skiing, is not enough. In addition to three to four hours a day of rigorous physical training and target

This swayed-back shooter's slouch permits the standing biathlete to rest one elbow against the chest for added stability and a more accurate aim.

practice, a top biathlete must develop extraordinary powers of self-control and concentration. Some employ sports psychologists; some practice biofeedback, yoga, or other forms of mental discipline, all in order to control and reduce their heart rates to about 120 beats per minute during shooting. Squeezing the trigger when the body is calmest—between breaths and some claim between heartbeats—the biathlete takes one or two breaths between shots. A biathlete hoping to win an Olympic medal should hit five out of five targets (at worst, four out of five) in each shooting sequence. It takes an expert thirty to forty-five seconds to shoot five targets with competitive accuracy.

EQUIPMENT

The Rifles

By regulation the rifles must be bolt action, fire .22-caliber long-rifle bullets, and weigh no less than 3.5 kilos (about 7.7 pounds). Large holes are often bored through the wooden stocks to reduce the rifle's weight to the minimum allowed.

At least 70 percent of all Olympic biathletes use an Anschutz rifle, preferably the much-lauded 1827 Fortner model, named for the Bavarian gunsmith who improved the bolt-action mechanism. Precision tooled, hand assembled, and perfectly balanced, each of these firearms costs about $3,000 and is crafted by Anschutz, a small firm in Germany.

While it is illegal to equip the gun with a magnifying lens or scope, most

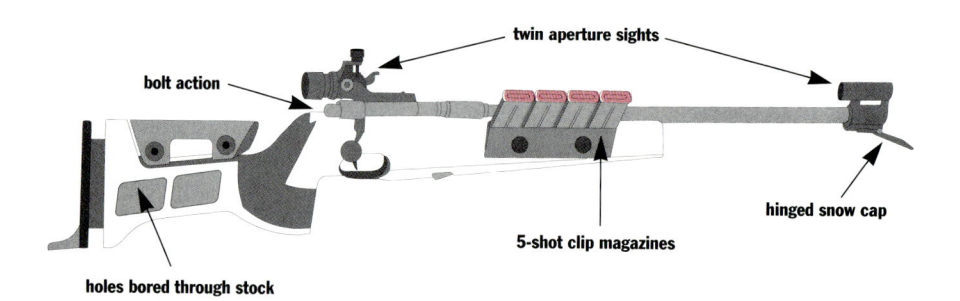

bolt action
twin aperture sights
hinged snow cap
5-shot clip magazines
holes bored through stock

Most rifles used in biathlon competitions share similar profiles and design elements, including twin aperture sights. Holes bored through the wooden stock reduce overall weight, an advantage when aiming the rifle and when carrying it on long, cross-country ski trails. As an option, the rifles can be fitted with convenient five-shot clip magazines on the forestock.

participants fit their rifles with an aperture sight, both front and rear. Each rifle has a double-loop strap, allowing the athlete to sling it over the shoulders while skiing.

Skis and Poles

The biathlete wears well-waxed and polished cross-country skis, which by regulation must be at least as long as the skier is tall. The skis attach to the boots with a hinged toe piece leaving the heel free (in Alpine skiing, both the heel and the toe are firmly attached to the ski). The ski poles, usually made of aluminum, are longer than those used for Alpine skiing. (See also: Cross-Country Skiing, page 94.)

The Targets

Set up 50 meters (164 feet) from the firing line, the targets are black steel disks, hinged at the bottom to flip down when hit (see illustration). From the standing position, the marksman shoots at targets measuring 115 millimeters in diameter (4 1/2 inches). In the prone position, where the rifle can be held steadier, the shooter must hit targets that measure just 45 mm across (1 3/4 inches, or about the size of a silver dollar).

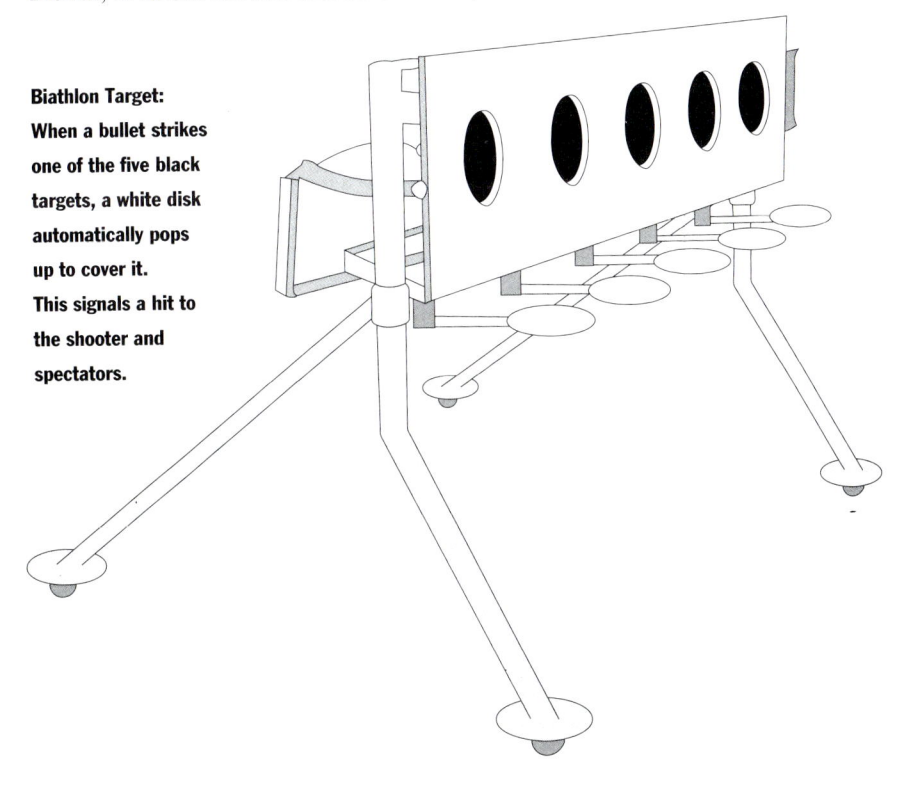

Biathlon Target: When a bullet strikes one of the five black targets, a white disk automatically pops up to cover it. This signals a hit to the shooter and spectators.

> At the 1972 Games in Japan, it snowed so hard that the biathlon had to be postponed. At the rifle range, the biathletes couldn't see, much less hit, the targets.

HISTORY

Although the modern biathlon is a relative newcomer to Winter Olympic medal competition (men's introduced in 1960, women's in 1992), the combining of the two skills dates back to the late nineteenth century in Scandinavian countries, where proficiency in rifle shooting and skiing was essential for hunters and border-patrol soldiers. The most famous of the original "biathletes" may have been the heroic Finnish soldiers of World War II, who, during the winter of 1940, camouflaged in snow-white uniforms, skied

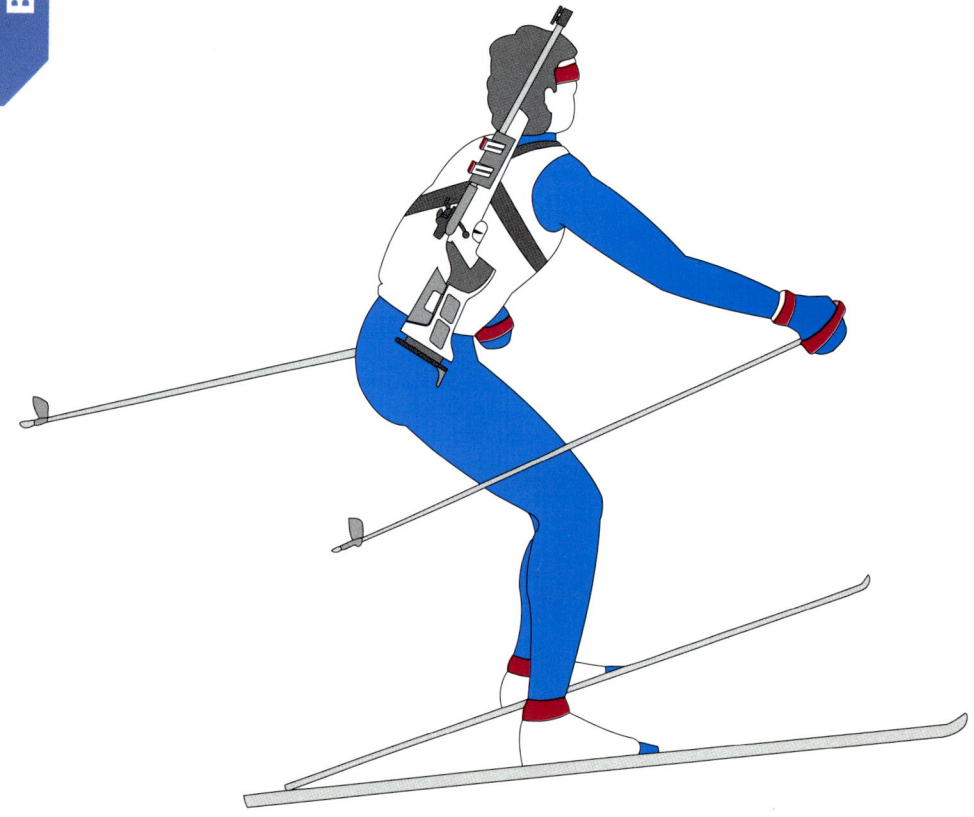

Although competitors are allowed to choose between the traditional classic style of cross-country skiing and the freestyle (or skating) method, virtually all biathletes today employ freestyle. Significantly faster, this method uses the basic body motion found in roller-skating or speedskating.

down mountainsides to make daring hit-and-run raids against invading Soviet troops.

The military heritage of the Olympic biathlon used to be even more evident in the competition. Until 1978, the rifles were of much larger caliber (up to 8 mm, or the equivalent of a big-game hunting rifle). Since the 1964 Games, the target distances have gradually been reduced from a maximum of 250 meters for some events to the present 50 meters for all events. To the dismay of Scandinavian traditionalists, mid-European countries (notably Italy, Austria, and Germany) instigated the revisions on the grounds that urban and suburban sprawl was elbowing out the shooting ranges big enough to accommodate the loud, large-caliber firearms. If less-powerful rifles had not been ordained by the sport's international ruling body, the biathletes from those countries would have had no convenient place to practice.

Since the biathlon was introduced as an Olympic sport, biathletes from Scandinavian countries, Germany, and the former Soviet Union have dominated Olympic competitions. Although U.S. competitors have improved their standings in recent years, they are not yet considered likely contenders for medals.

Not only must successful biathletes have the stamina of marathon runners, they also must be able to calm their heart rates immediately after skiing in order to shoot their .22-caliber target rifles accurately.

BOBSLED • 20

Bobsled

Rocketing down a white chute of ice at nearly 100 miles an hour, the modern Olympic bobsled seems capable of launching itself and its helmeted crew into outer space. A muffled roar signals its approach as the sled rips through the curves on the upper track and builds speed on the straightaways. Then, bullet-like, it flashes by in a bright blur of color, vanishing around the next high-banked bend.

There are two types of races in this Olympic sport: two- and four-man bobsled competitions. In a two-man sled, there are the driver, or "pilot," and the brakeman. In the four-man, the crew also includes two pushmen. There is no women's competition.

One at a time, the bobsleds race down the track, or "run," which is a trough of ice no less than 1,500 meters long (about .9 of a mile). Gaining speed as they go, the sleds reach top speeds of 80–90 mph. At these speeds, a competitive run is over in about 56 seconds. In the Olympics each team makes four runs, the times are added together, and the team with the lowest combined time wins the event.

Although there are separate tracks at Lake Placid, international bobsled races are usually held on the same track as the luge; forks at the beginning of the run create event-specific starting ramps. The entire run usually includes about a dozen banked curves, at least one of which must be an S-curve. Many have a "labyrinth," which is a set of three consecutive curves. And some of the newer tracks feature what is called a "kreisel," a 270-degree loop that produces a G-force of about 4.5. At four-and-one-half times normal gravity, it becomes difficult for the driver to keep his head up and to steer the sled.

RACING THE BOBRUN

To begin a race, the team members take their positions beside the sled and grasp the push bars, slide the sled a step forward, then back, and then with all their might heave forward and push it for a good fifty yards. In a two-man sled, the driver jumps in first, followed by the brakeman. In the four-man, the driver is followed by the two pushmen and then the brakeman. Getting aboard quickly, smoothly, and without rocking the sled is difficult and takes

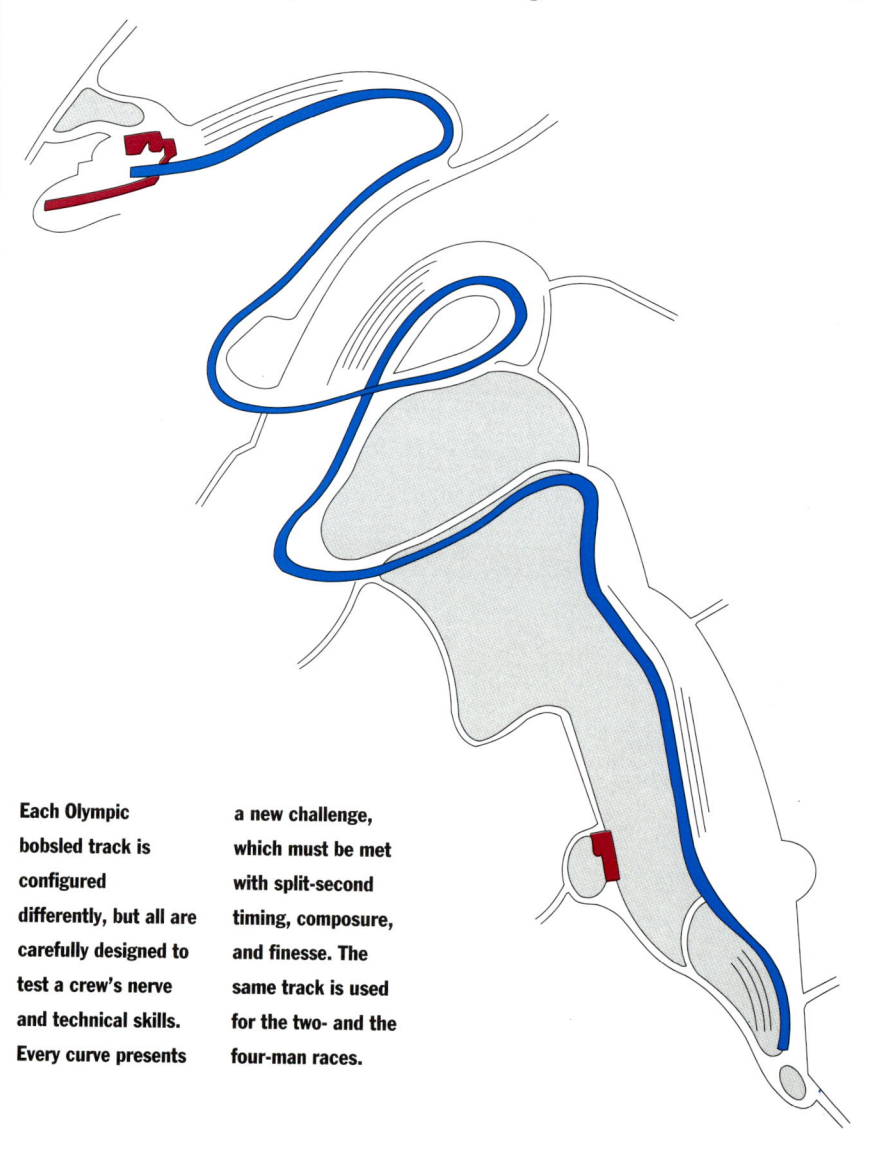

Each Olympic bobsled track is configured differently, but all are carefully designed to test a crew's nerve and technical skills. Every curve presents a new challenge, which must be met with split-second timing, composure, and finesse. The same track is used for the two- and the four-man races.

plenty of team practice, especially in the four-man event.

Once aboard, the driver immediately snaps down his retractable push bar, which collapses flush with the body. He then reaches forward for the two D-rings, which are metal handles connected to a pulley mechanism that allows the driver to steer the sled by turning the front runners to the left or the right. The other team members must also retract their push bars and hold onto metal hand grips on the floor for the duration of the race. Crouching low in the racing position, the bobsledders, or "sliders," keep their heads bowed to minimize wind resistance (and some say to pray).

After the push start the race rests in the steady hands of the pilot, who must replace prerace anxieties with calm nerves and quick, yet calculating reflexes. Having previously studied every twist and turn on the run, he gingerly works the D-rings, centering the speeding sled on the straightaways and

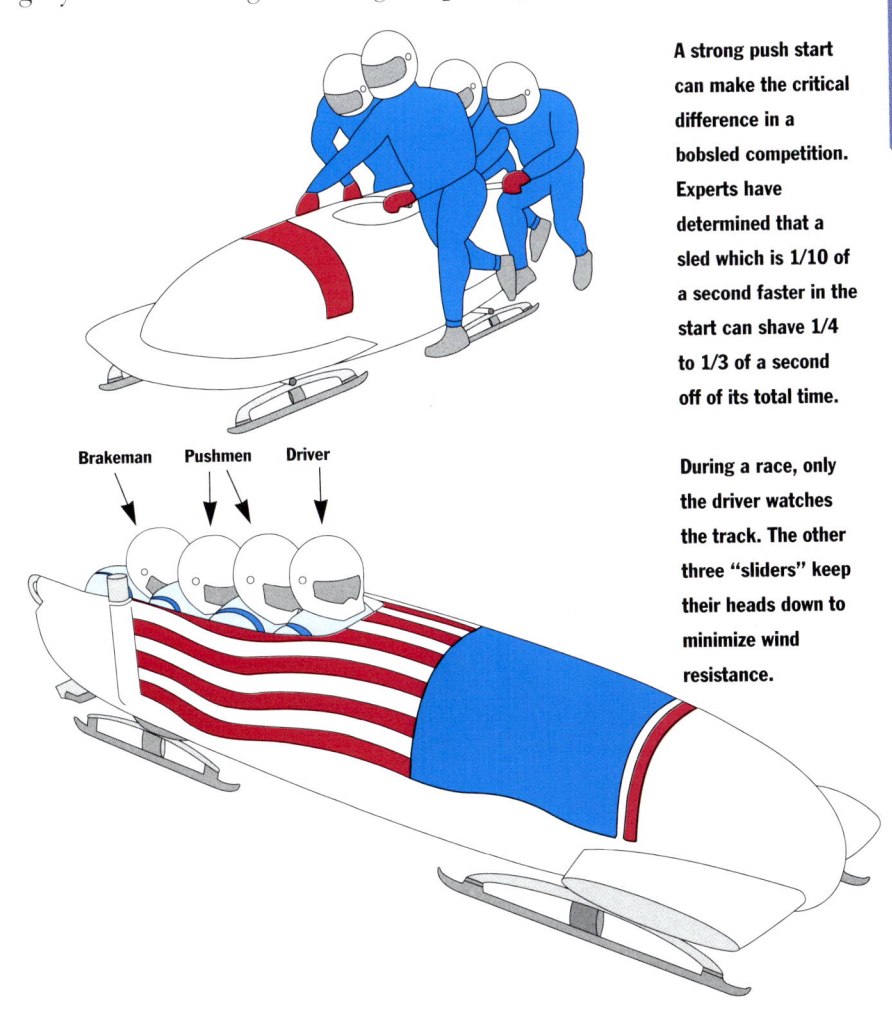

A strong push start can make the critical difference in a bobsled competition. Experts have determined that a sled which is 1/10 of a second faster in the start can shave 1/4 to 1/3 of a second off of its total time.

Brakeman   Pushmen   Driver

During a race, only the driver watches the track. The other three "sliders" keep their heads down to minimize wind resistance.

keeping it away from the walls that can dramatically slow it down. Attempting to enter each curve at just the right angle, the pilot makes split-second adjustments in the turns, gently releasing the rings as the sled shoots out of a curve and into the next section of track like a runaway roller coaster.

The other team members help guide and balance the sled by shifting their weight in the curves. At the end of the race, it is the brakeman's job to slow and stop the sled, something that he rarely, if ever, does during the race itself.

Strategically, the driver tries to approach each curve from the outside and take the bank a little above center for maximum speed and for the best track position coming out of the turn. Should he come into a curve on the inside (called "taking the curve late"), the sled will have a tendency to climb too high on the embankment and possibly slam into the overhang, which keeps

Line A is the optimum course for the bobsled to take on a fast, high-banking curve in the track. Approaching from the outside, the sled will have a tendency to climb about halfway up the banked turn, maintain momentum, and complete the turn in the middle of the track. Line B shows a sled "taking the curve late." The inside approach will propel the sled up too high on the bank, probably causing it to slam into the upper retaining wall and then into the lower wall as it exits the curve—causing significant loss of speed and time.

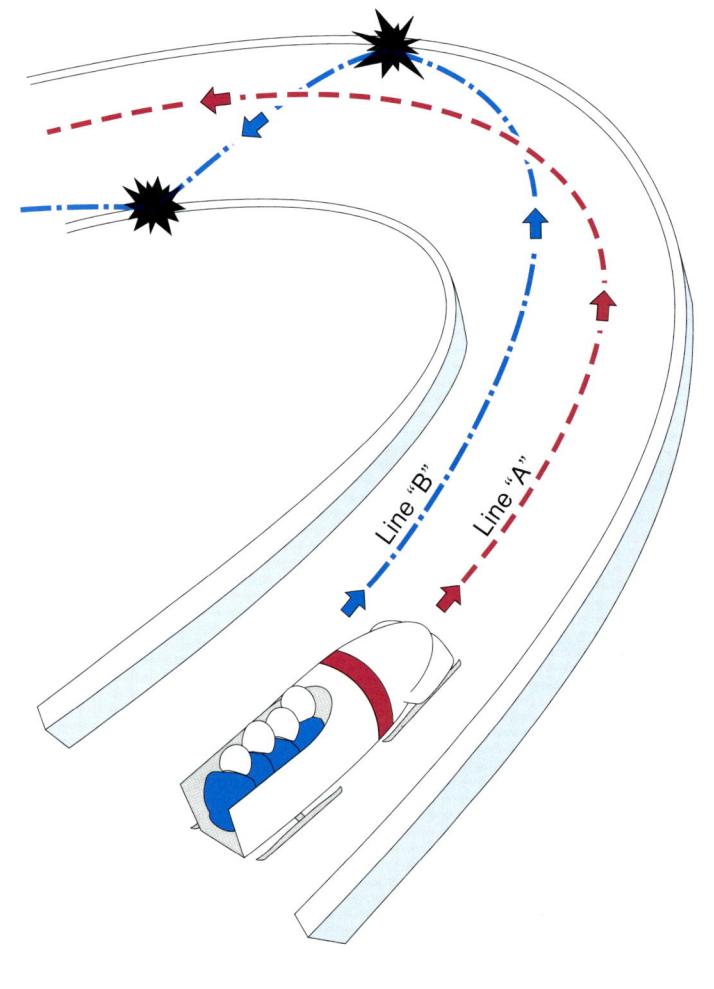

the sled from vaulting over the wall. This can prove disastrous by overturning the sled. If the sled ricochets off the lip but proceeds out of the curve right-side up, it will likely veer across the track and slam against the inside wall. Usually, the sled will continue down the run, but it will have lost valuable time and momentum.

Should the sled overturn, most coaches instruct their sliders to try to remain in the sled and maintain the heads-down racing posture. At such high speeds the sled can actually protect the athletes from ice burns and often from serious injury. One of the biggest dangers to a crew member is to be thrown out and ahead of the sled in a curve where the sled's weight and velocity can prove fatal.

COMPETITORS

Sports Illustrated once characterized bobsledders as "scarfaced, gimlet-eyed, speed-demented daredevils." And until recent years, that pretty much summed them up. But by the 1970s, Olympic bobsledding was becoming more serious, and coaches began recruiting more carefully. They scouted the ranks of colleges and universities for accomplished track-and-field athletes who could power the bobsleds in those all-important push starts. Drivers also trained harder by taking more practice runs to master their essential skills.

The seventies and eighties were also an era of rapid technological advancement in bobsled design and construction, particularly in East Germany, the U.S., and the Soviet Union. Motivated by space-age discoveries and Cold War competitiveness, government, university, and corporate scientists and engineers began an exorbitantly expensive "techno-race" to develop highly sophisticated designs with structural and mechanical advantages for their Olympic bobsledders. The Germans, for example, gained an edge with the introduction of independent suspension and a two-part rear axle. Others experimented with Teflon and silicon coatings on the runners to enhance speed. NASA's wind tunnels were used to test sled aerodynamics, and computer simulations were employed to test various weight and surface friction combinations.

Concern arose that advantages such as these threatened to overshadow the athlete's role in bobsledding and give advantage to high-tech countries. So in several heroic steps backward, beginning in the late eighties, bobsledding's international governing body outlawed many of these modern "improvements" and imposed stricter guidelines in an effort to protect the integrity of the sport and to keep the focus on athletic ability.

With the restrictions on sled design and construction, coaches and teams zeroed in on developing better drivers and, especially, on strengthening the

BOBSLED • 26

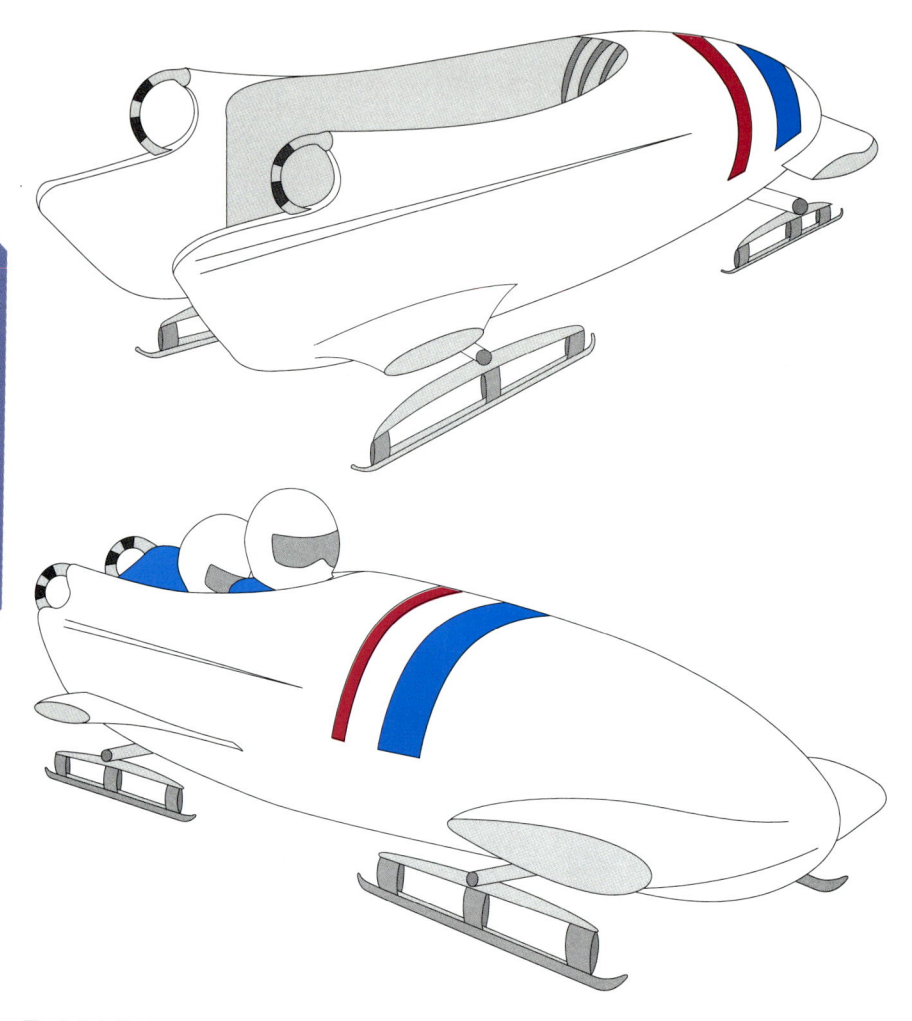

The bobsled's sleek design is strictly for speed. It can travel up to 80–90 miles an hour, and a race down an Olympic bobrun takes less than a minute. A two-man bobsled, however, must be guided more than the larger, heavier four-man sled. The difference between them has been compared to driving a dune buggy and a Cadillac.

Eddie Eagan is the only person ever to win a gold medal in both the Summer and the Winter Olympics. He won the light heavyweight boxing championship at the 1920 Summer Olympics, and in 1932 he was a member of the winning U.S. four-man bobsled team.

push starts to gain an advantage. The starts are important because momentum established at the start will accumulate speed throughout the run. A sled that is 1/10 of a second faster in the start can shave 1/4 to 1/3 of a second off the total run time.

Bobsledders, therefore, need to be strong, particularly in the legs for the push. Typically, a driver is about 5'10", 185–95 pounds. A brakeman stands about 6'1", 195–205 pounds; and pushmen are the strongest, about 6', 200–205 pounds.

Training concentrates not so much on endurance but on building explosive power, as might be seen in a football running back. Exercise regimens call for sprints, jumping, and work with free weights, which includes numerous squats with about three hundred pounds across the shoulders.

Although bobsledders do not ordinarily train in their sport for as many years as other Olympic athletes, experience does count. A lot. Most participants start as pushers, then graduate to brakemen with aspirations to become drivers. Once a driver, it usually takes a good three years of racing experience to become competitive on the international level.

EQUIPMENT

The Sleds

Sleek, shiny, and bullet-like with tapered fins both fore and aft, the sleds themselves are often the central attraction for spectators and participants alike at Olympic bobsled competitions.

The two-man sled measures about ten feet from end to end versus about twelve feet for the four-man sled. Most bobsleds are composed of a steel chassis and fiberglass body riding on two sets of steel runners, moveable in front and stationary in the rear. The body is actually in two parts—with the break just in front of the driver—so that the sled can bend with the curves and be more easily maneuvered.

The fin-like projections are actually bumpers to protect the sled from slamming against the walls and have little or no aerodynamic value. The brake is nothing more than a steel, rakelike arm that, when the brakeman pulls up on a lever, drops down from the belly of the sled to claw at the ice and slow the vehicle.

There are, of course, big weight differences between the two types of sleds. Weighing about 600 pounds empty, the four-man cannot exceed 1,388 pounds with all four Olympians aboard. The two-man sled weighs about 440 pounds; the two occupants cannot add more than an additional 419 pounds.

The differences in weight and length have tremendous bearing on the sleds' racing behaviors. "One drives like a dune buggy," says a coach for the U.S. team, "and the other like a Cadillac." The lighter weight, two-man sled is less stable and can get into trouble faster on the track, but it is also more responsive to the driver. The heavier four-man sled, on the other hand, is smoother and glides better. But if it starts to tip or skid, the big sled can quickly become uncontrollable.

Costs? A two-man, Olympic-caliber sled carries a price tag of about $18,000 to $20,000. The four-man costs between $23,000 and $25,000. But prototypes built by wealthy, technologically minded countries can cost a half-million dollars or more.

Racing Gear

All Olympic bobsledders must wear helmets, and most choose top-of-the-line motorcycle helmets with goggles instead of face shields because goggles fog up less. Their body suits are typically made of Lycra with a polyurethane coating to minimize wind resistance. To aid in the push starts, participants wear special shoes with hundreds of needlelike spikes on the soles to give added traction on the ice.

The Track

Bobsled runs are long, curving troughs of ice with sharply banked turns. The ice is manufactured using a network of refrigeration pipes beneath the track. These usually contain an ammonia-based coolant that freezes water sprayed on the surface. During an event, track surface grooming and repair are important because the heavy sleds tend to rut and chip the ice. Attendants shovel filler slush onto rough spots, smoothing the areas out with trowels before the filler freezes.

A bobsledder's shoe provides traction on the ice for the important push-starts. The needle-like spikes can be dangerous, so team members must be careful where they step when jumping aboard the sled.

HISTORY

The forerunner of the bobsled was the ancient toboggan, which was used to haul loads across the snow. It was not until the 1870s, in St. Moritz, Switzerland, that the first run was built specifically for bobsled races. At about the same time, bobsleds were also becoming popular in Canada. In those days, a bobsled was essentially two sleds joined together end to end with the front runners moveable and the rear ones stationary.

The earliest bobsled competitions were held in St. Moritz in the 1880s, and four-man bobsleds were included in the first Winter Olympics in 1924 (Chamonix). That year, Switzerland won the gold, followed by Germany and Belgium.

It was not until the 1932 Olympics (Lake Placid) that the two-man bobsled event was included. The American team won the two-man competition that year, mainly because the sliders heated the runners with a blowtorch for twenty-five minutes before the race. Today, it's highly illegal to heat the runners before a race; back then, it was considered unusual but acceptable.

Over the past twenty years, virtually all Olympic medals for bobsledding events have been captured by German and Swiss teams. Other good teams have heralded from the former Soviet Union, Austria, Italy, and the U.S.

It takes a nervy driver, quick reflexes, and steady concentration to guide a speeding bobsled down a trough of gleaming white ice. The smallest error can decide a race.

FIGURE SKATING • 30

Figure Skating

From explosive jumps to graceful spirals across the gleaming ice, figure skating is a special feature of every Winter Olympics. There is nothing quite so enthralling as the solitary skaters on the frozen rink, giving their all to the powerful music of Wagner, Chopin, or Rodgers and Hammerstein.

Winning performances in Olympic figure skating must be both lyrical and dazzling. The three events are: the singles competition for both men and women, pair skating, and ice dancing. All are held on an ice rink measuring at least 200 x 85 feet, often the same rink used for ice hockey. Nine judges preside over each event, and in the performances they look for excellent form, accomplished technique, gracefulness, and passionate energy.

SINGLES

Considered to be one of the most difficult winter sports to master, singles figure skating is a captivating blend of grace, strength, precise timing, and the nerve of a soloist. In the finals of Olympic competition, singles skaters must perform a short, or "technical," program and a long, or "freestyle," program. Each skater usually performs one program a day on two consecutive days.

The short program is performed first and counts one-third of the skater's overall score. It can take no more than two minutes and forty seconds to perform, and each skater is required to execute a total of eight specified steps, jumps, and on-ice spins for the judges to appraise.

The freestyle program, the second part of singles competition, lasts four-and-a-half minutes for men and four minutes for women. Calling for a more innovative performance than the short program, it counts two-thirds of the skater's overall score. The rules require that the program include a balanced

FIGURE SKATING • 32

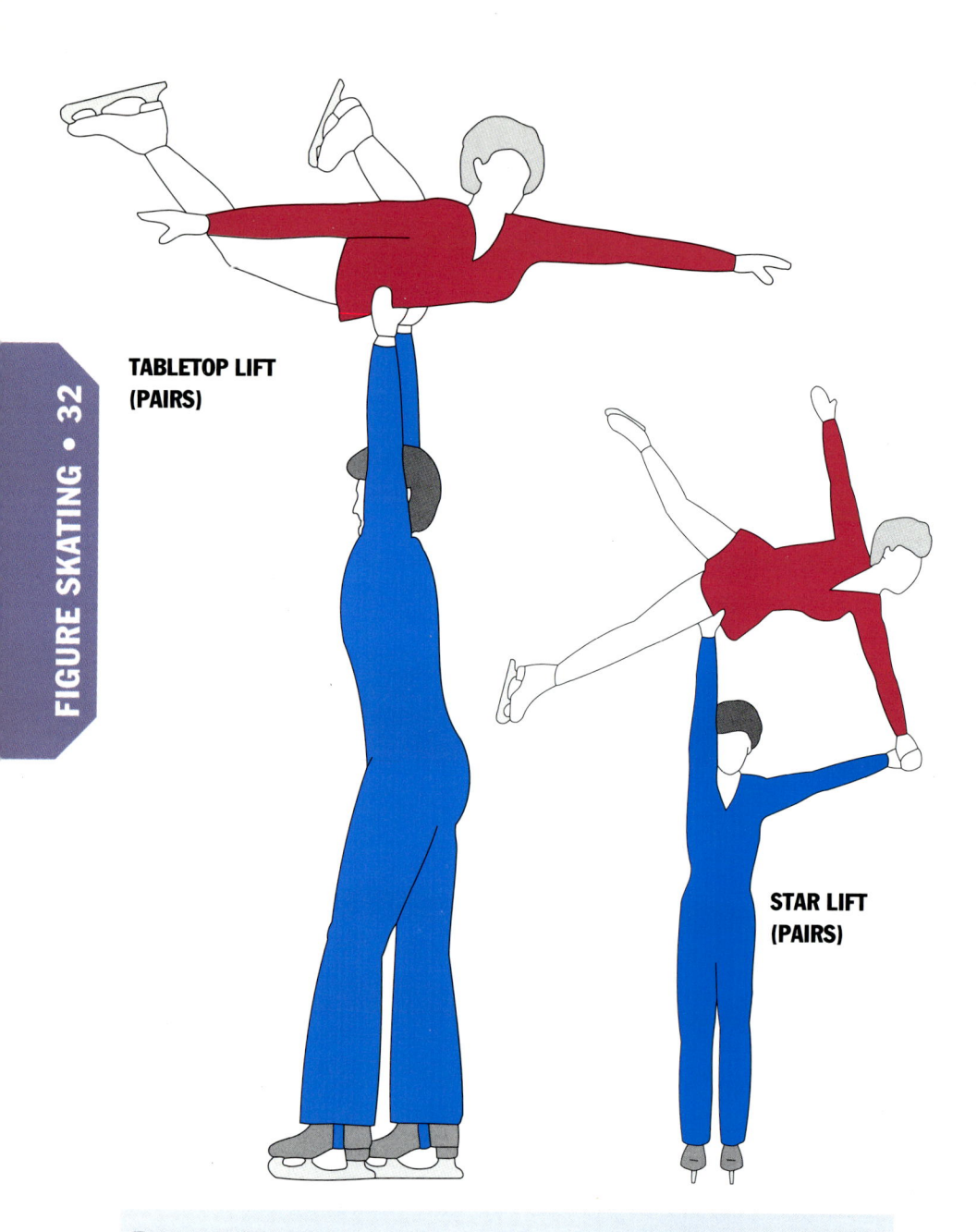

TABLETOP LIFT (PAIRS)

STAR LIFT (PAIRS)

To improve their performance during an event, many top athletes employ a technique called "visual imagery." Just before the event, the athlete takes a few moments to form a mental picture of himself or herself performing exceptionally well throughout the event and of winning it.

number of jumps and spins, but because it is "freestyle," there is no stipulation as to which moves must be performed.

For both the short and long programs, the skater selects his or her own music. The music, however, must be strictly instrumental; no vocals are permitted. Usually, skaters select traditional music—classical pieces or sometimes scores from popular musicals—with varying tempos and moods to demonstrate a wide range of skating talent and interpretive skills, from exciting, daring, and athletic to serene, graceful, and beautifully controlled.

For each program, the skater is judged both on technical merit (how accurately each move or jump is executed and its level of difficulty) and on artistic merit (sometimes called the "composition and style" score, which evaluates the athlete's presentation of the program). Scoring is on a scale of 1 to 6, with 6 representing a perfect performance. The two scores are then combined for a total score. Excellent scores range from 5.5 to the rare 6.0.

PAIRS

In some respects, pair skating is even more demanding than singles, and it is certainly more complicated because the pair's movements must be harmonious and often in unison.

Like singles, the two-day pair skating competition is divided into a short and a long program, lasting two minutes and forty seconds and four-and-a-half minutes respectively. The short program counts one-third of the total

SIT SPIN (PAIRS)

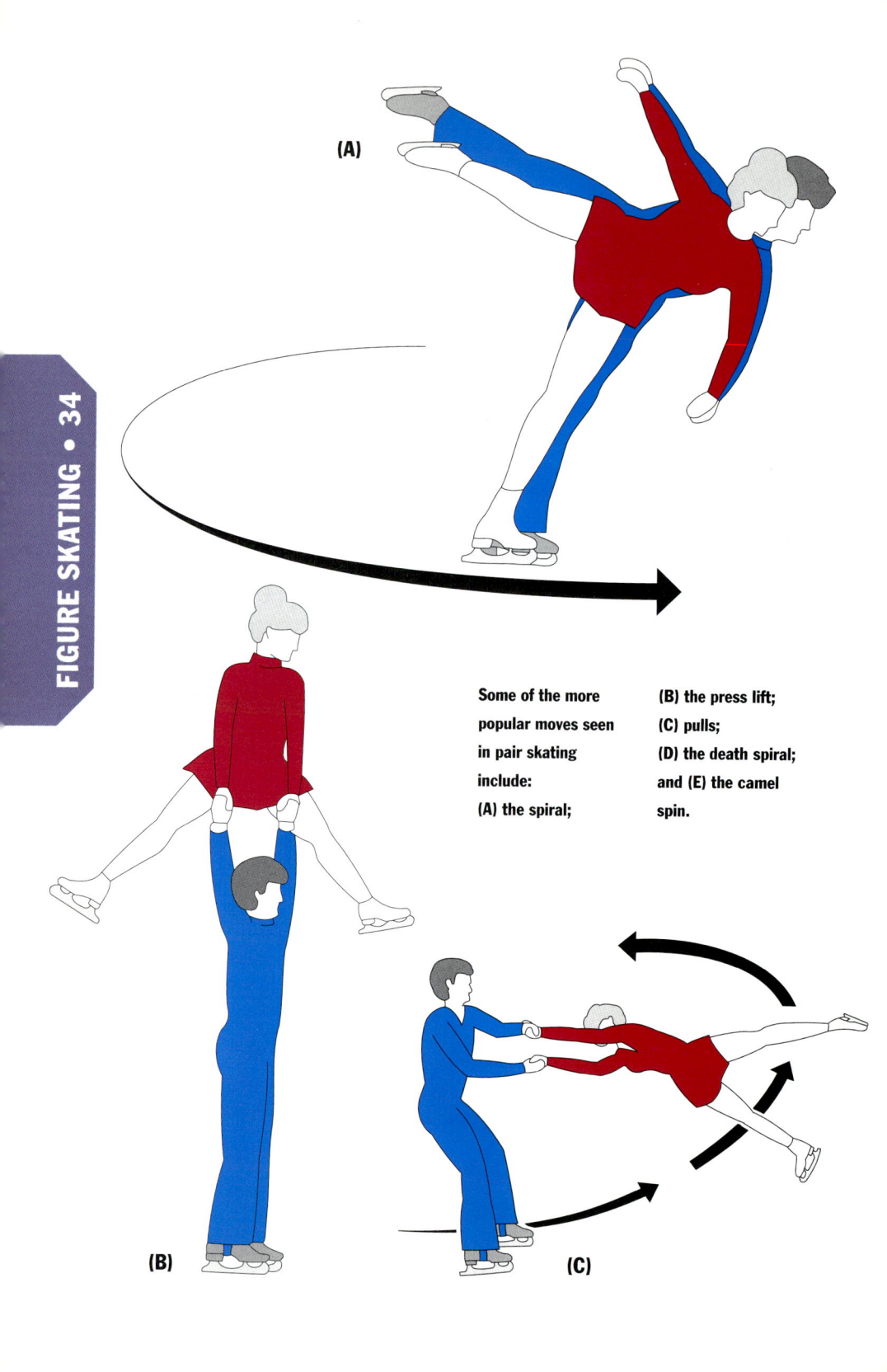

FIGURE SKATING • 34

Some of the more popular moves seen in pair skating include:
(A) the spiral;
(B) the press lift;
(C) pulls;
(D) the death spiral;
and (E) the camel spin.

After capturing the gold medal for figure skating in 1984, German skater Katarina Witt received thirty-five thousand love letters from around the world.

(D)

(E)

FIGURE SKATING • 35

score, the long two-thirds. And, like singles, the nine judges score each performance two ways—first for technical merit and then for artistic merit—on a scale of 1 to 6. The music must be instrumental and is selected by the athletes.

Because pair skaters are able to execute a wider variety of moves than singles, including overhead lifts and partner-assisted jumps, the programs provide spectators with a greater diversity of jumps and spins. The moves can also involve a greater element of risk for the athletes, particularly for the woman, who is often hoisted high over her partner's head or hurled through the air in spectacular throw jumps. With nothing but ice to break her fall, the potential for serious injury is significant.

Pair skaters strive to be appreciated as unified elements of a single performance, a partnership of grace and fluid motion. When spins and jumps are executed, judges prefer to see them done in perfect synchronization. These enchanting portions of the performances are sometimes called shadow or mirror skating.

Also important to the judges is the undefinable bond between pair skaters, that chemistry which the great champions seem to exude naturally, as if they were born to skate together. This special on-ice relationship communicates zest, harmony, and romance and takes successful pair skaters years to develop and perfect.

ICE DANCING

If the on-ice relationship between pair skaters appears romantic, then the relationship between ice dancers can be downright sensual. Introduced as a medal event in 1976 (Innsbruck), ice dancing is also the Winter Olympic sport that strays furthest away from athletics toward art. And because ice dancing entails so much artistry, it is the most subjective and therefore most difficult form of figure skating for a judging panel to evaluate.

Although artistic interpretation is a fundamental aspect of ice dancing, there are restrictions imposed on the skaters—the guiding rule being that whatever dance the skaters choose to perform on ice must be roughly translatable to a dance floor. Originality of dance moves is expected and highly regarded, so unlike singles or pair skating, ice dancing involves very few nameable poses or moves.

Ice dancing is composed of three competitive programs: the compulsory dances, the original dance, and the free dance. For all three programs, the dancers must be in physical contact for the entire performance, except briefly for a quick change of position or hold. Lifts and jumps are not permitted in the compulsory and original programs.

In the compulsory dances, the first program of the competition, virtually

In a speech given in 1894, Baron Pierre de Coubertin, the father of the modern Olympics, declared, "The most important thing in the Olympic Games is not to win but to take part, just as the most important thing in life is not the triumph but the struggle. The essential thing is not to have conquered but to have fought well." These words were adopted as the official Olympic creed.

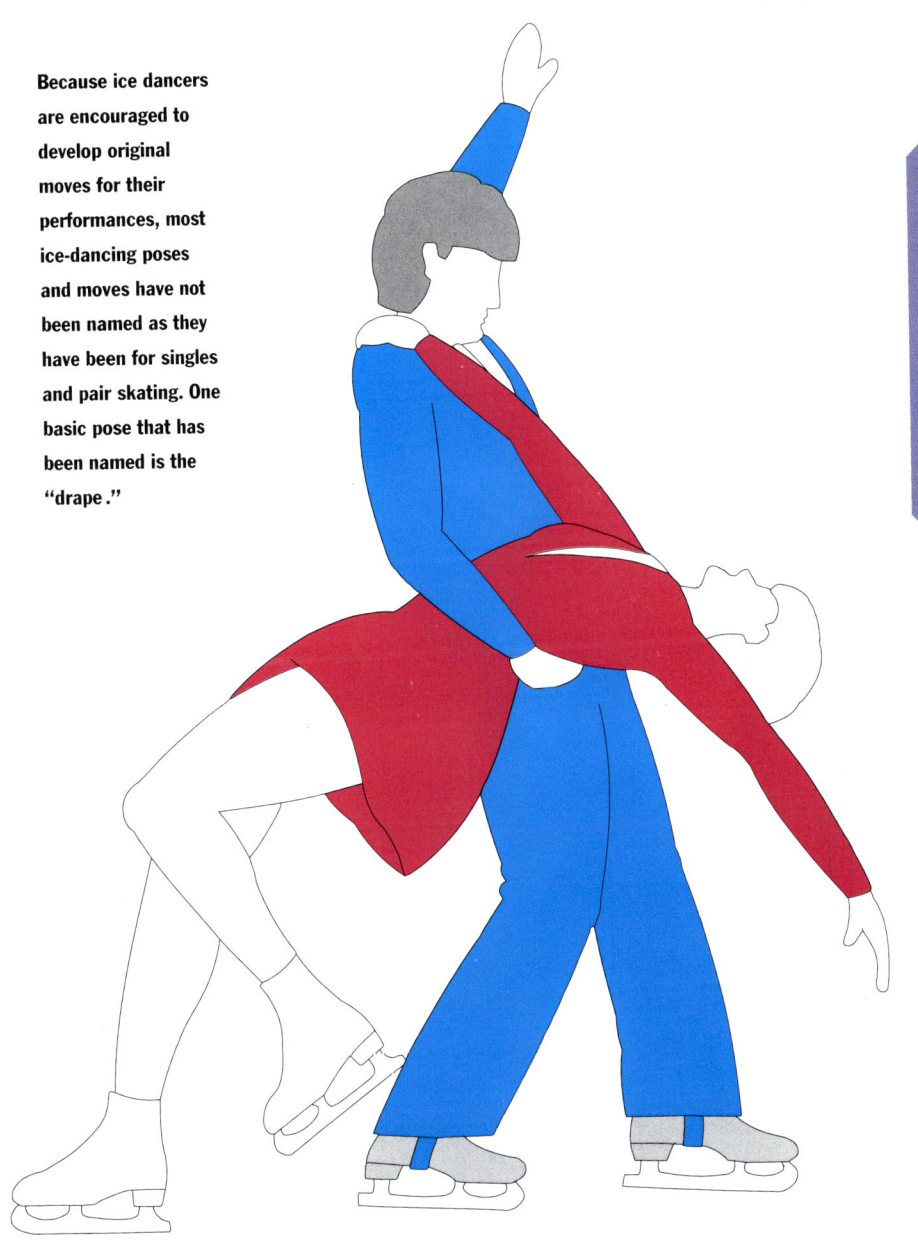

Because ice dancers are encouraged to develop original moves for their performances, most ice-dancing poses and moves have not been named as they have been for singles and pair skating. One basic pose that has been named is the "drape."

everything—including the music—is dictated by the rules, and must be followed precisely by the couples. Each couple must perform two different types of dances (such as the fox-trot, polka, waltz, rhumba, etc.) that have been preselected by the officials and entail specified on-ice patterns. The official rule book shows diagrams of each pattern, and coaches and skaters memorize and practice them. Each dance lasts about a minute and then immediately must be repeated exactly as it was performed the first time. Accuracy of the steps and placement of the patterns are critical. Together, the compulsory dances count 20 percent of a couple's overall score.

The second part of the competition is the original dance. This program consists of one dance, lasting two minutes, and counts 30 percent of the overall score. The dance rhythm or beat is prescribed by the officials, but the music, program, and choreography are left to the skaters. The officials prescribe the rhythm two years in advance to give skaters, coaches, and choreographers enough time to plan and prepare.

Given on the scale of 1 to 6, the score for technical merit covers difficulty and correct execution of dance steps, flow of the performance, and variety. The score for artistic merit, also ranging from 1 to 6, takes into account style, unity, creative interpretation, as well as a sense of timing and rhythm. These

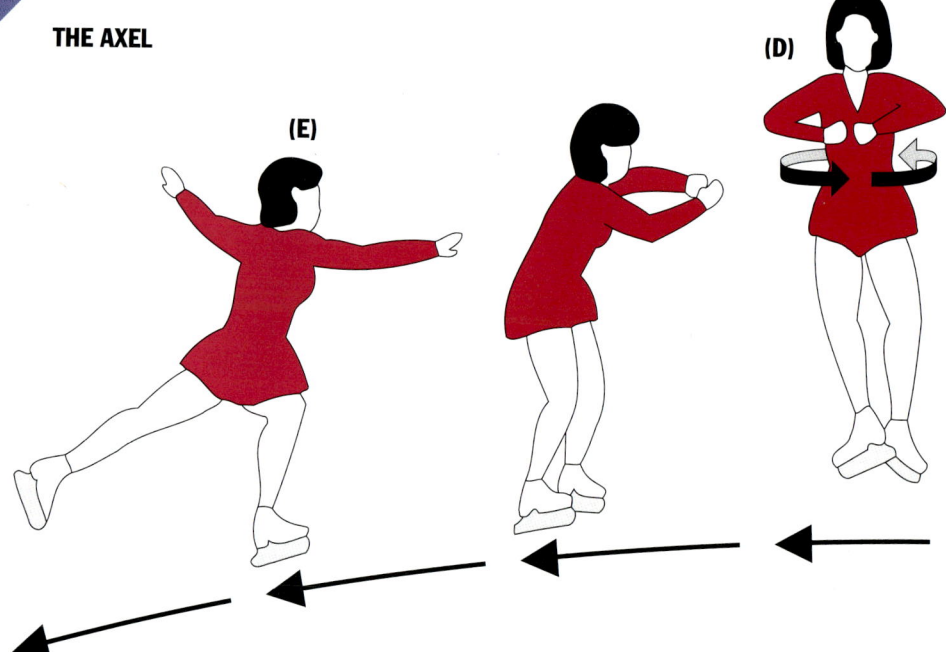

THE AXEL

two scores are then combined for one overall score.

Free dance is the third and final program of the ice dancing competition. This segment lasts four minutes, counts 50 percent of a couple's overall rating, and is judged on technical and artistic merits. The free-dance program permits skaters the broadest artistic interpretation of dance music and allows a set number of lifts (no more than shoulder high) and jumps (no more than one revolution in the air).

In the free-dance program, judges tend to reward more difficult footwork, a variety of moves, fresh and original musical interpretation (choreography), a sense of unity and style from the couple, and a strong sense of musical expression and feeling. Originality, creativity, and expression count the most in the free-dance program.

JUMPS

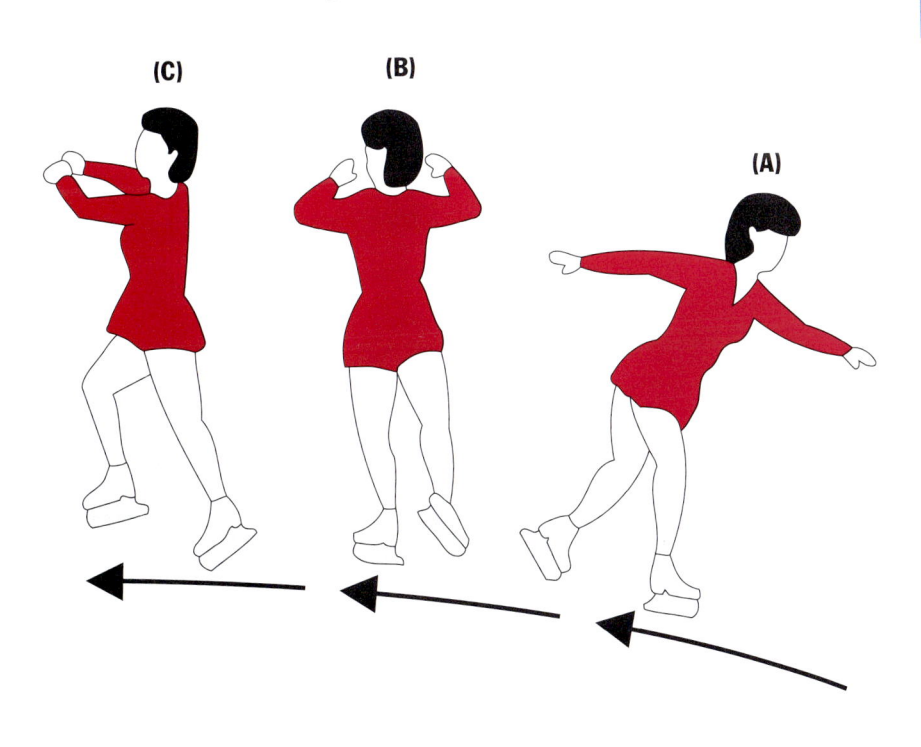

There are dozens upon dozens of possible moves in men's and women's figure skating, from the subtleties of foot and hand positioning to sensational jumps. Most jumps are executed so fast that it is often difficult for spectators to differentiate one from another. In singles competition, the height achieved is based on the power of the skater's legs. In pair skating, however, the male skater can give extra lift to his partner by hurling her into the air in spinning jumps that are spectacular to witness; these are called "throw jumps."

Rotational jumps (those that include in-air rotation) like the Axel, Lutz, and Salchow are produced by the skater's forward momentum, upward leap, and quick, precisely timed turn of the head, arms, shoulders, and outside leg, allowing the athlete to spin in the air before landing. Unlike the limited potential of a person running on dry land who jumps up to rotate, the ice skater has the advantage of using the skates as a moving platform. This enables the athlete to maintain speed while bending the legs deeply to attain maximum thrust from the quadriceps, producing a stronger upward leap. On land, an athlete has to plant one or both feet before springing upward, causing a great loss of forward momentum. Skaters also have the capacity to transfer all of the energy back to the skates upon landing, allowing for the smoothest possible transition between air and ice.

Successful, multirotational jumps begin with a strong take-off from the right or left skate; the higher the better. The free leg is often used to generate extra power and height by kicking up as the skater leaps from the on-ice skate. Simultaneously, the skater swings both outstretched arms in the direction of the rotation to generate more power and more revolutions. Once airborne, rotation can be made even faster by drawing the fists to the chest and crossing the legs.

Skaters always land on one skate, usually the right, going backwards. To stop, or "check," the rotation upon landing the skater brings both arms out wide. Once the touch-down blade contacts the ice, the free leg is immediately swung straight back to check rotation further and to establish stability and balance.

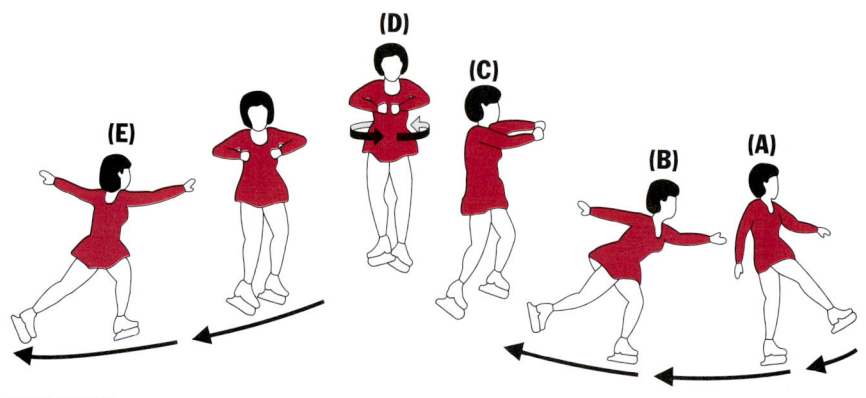

THE LUTZ

The Axel (See illustration, pages 38–39.)

Considered to be the most difficult jump in figure skating, this challenging move was originated in 1882 by Norwegian figure and speedskating champion Axel Paulsen. Properly executed, the Axel is a very dramatic jump and a real crowd (and judge) pleaser. Unlike most jumps, in the Axel the skater jumps forward and up, pushing off from the outside edge of the left skate blade.

While skating backwards, the competitor approaches the jump in a broad, counterclockwise arc. Just before the jump (A) the skater glides on the right skate—still going backwards—then (B) steps forcefully around onto the left skate. Bending deeply at the knee, the skater leaps (C) kicking upward with the free right leg and rotating shoulders, arms, and head to the left. This unified motion lifts the jumper into the air (D) in a counterclockwise rotation.

For a single Axel, the skater does one-and-a-half revolutions and lands (E) on the right skate going backwards. To perform a double or triple Axel, the skater must jump higher and pull the fists into the chest more quickly to generate a faster rotation and more revolutions in the air.

The Lutz (See illustration, opposite page.)

Invented by Austrian skater Alois Lutz in the 1930s, the Lutz is a spectacular jump and a popular staple in Olympic competitions. It is generally considered the second most difficult jump to execute. Like the Axel, skaters do single, double, or triple rotations in the air.

While skating backwards (A) the athlete approaches the Lutz on a clockwise arc—unusual because most jumps are approached going counterclockwise. Shifting weight to the left foot (B) the skater bends at the knee, draws the right skate underneath, and (C) powers the leap up with the left leg and a quick assist from the toe pick of the right skate. (D) After one counterclockwise revolution in the air—for a single—the performer (E) lands on the right skate going backwards in a counterclockwise arc.

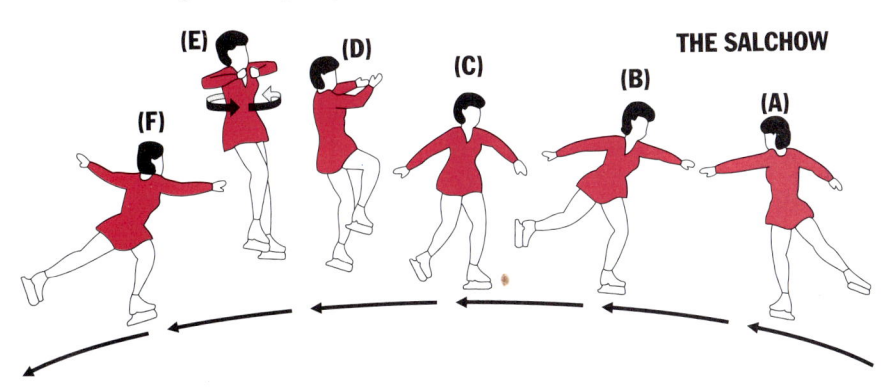

THE SALCHOW

The Salchow (See illustration, page 41.)

This jump (pronounced sal-kow) was created by Ulrich Salchow, a Swedish champion who dominated figure skating during the first decade of the twentieth century.

(A) Skating forward on the left skate in a counterclockwise arc, the competitor (B) hops a half-revolution around (called a 3-turn) and is now skating backwards—still on the left foot. (C) Bending at the knee, the skater springs up from the left skate (D) while kicking up with the free right leg, (E) rotates a revolution counterclockwise, and (F) lands going backwards on the right skate. Because this jump requires so much muscle power, spectators see more double than triple Salchows.

The Flip

This jump is similar to the Salchow, but because the skater gains an assist by digging in, or "planting," with the right toe pick and springing up from both skates, some skaters say the flip is not quite as difficult as the Salchow.

The Loop

Sometimes called a Rittberger in Europe, the loop jump was originated at the turn of the century by Werner Rittberger.

As with most other jumps, the skater (A) approaches the loop while skating backwards in a counterclockwise arc. (B) Stepping onto the right skate—still going backwards—the competitor twists the shoulders and outstretched arms to the right, extending the free left leg slightly forward, then bends the right leg and (C) leaps up while twisting left into (D) a counterclockwise rotation and crossing the left leg over the right. One full revolution is performed in the air before (E) coming back down on the right skate. Upon touchdown, the competitor (F) swings the free left leg behind and throws the arms straight out to the sides in order to "check" or stop the rotation and to regain balance quickly on the ice.

Because the free left leg does not aid the jump by kicking up at the start of

THE LOOP

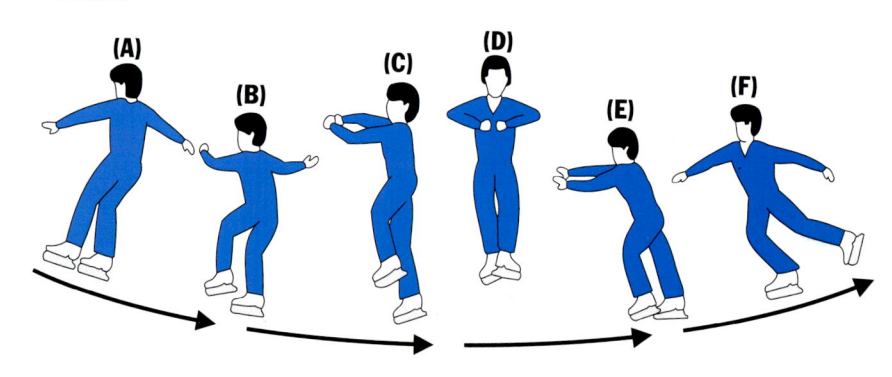

the leap, the loop jump is considered more difficult than the Salchow. The entire jump is powered only by the right leg, so a triple loop is a rarity.

The Toe Loop

The toe loop differs from the loop in that the skater uses the left toe pick for an added boost while jumping off the right leg. It is, therefore, usually considered an easier jump to execute.

OTHER POPULAR MOVES

In addition to jumps, skaters also execute an array of spins and spirals to enhance their dynamic performances. In an on-ice spin, the skater revolves on a central point while maintaining a specific pose. In a spiral, the skater strikes a certain pose while gliding (usually on one skate) in a long, arcing line across the ice. So a specific pose, the "camel" for example, can be executed as a "camel spin" and as a "spiral" in the camel pose.

Camel Spin and Flying Camel

First performed in 1935 by British champion Cecelia Colledge, the camel spin is derived from a ballet move, the arabesque.

The camel is approached while skating backwards on one skate. Then, with arms wide, the skater twists gracefully while stepping onto the other

THE CAMEL SPIN

skate and into a tight spin, stretching the free leg to the rear and both arms out and parallel with the ice.

The flying camel, attributed to Dick Button, concludes with the camel spin but is enhanced by a more dramatic entrance. For this jump, the skater begins the approach by going backwards, usually on the right skate with the left leg extended behind. Twisting counterclockwise, the competitor steps

THE LAYBACK

forward onto the left skate, followed by a strong, counterclockwise sweep of the free right leg and simultaneous spring upward off the left skate. This motion carries the skater up in the air, with the torso parallel to the ice and the legs in somewhat of a scissor kick. Landing on the right skate, the left leg is extended back, and the skater revolves in a classic camel spin.

The Layback

The layback begins with a traditional in-place, upright spin on the left skate. Then the skater slowly arches the back and tilts back the head. This lovely move, a favorite in the women's event, was created by Cecelia Colledge, the same skater who invented the camel spin.

The Sit Spin

A difficult move for some skaters, the sit spin requires powerful leg muscles for the deep knee bend—usually done with the left skate on the ice. The spin is counterclockwise and with the right leg fully extended and parallel to the ice. The hard part comes when it is time to rise without touching the right skate to the ice. This move was developed by American Jackson Haines (see History, page 48).

WHY SKATERS FALL

Most falls can be traced to poorly executed take-offs rather than faulty landings. If the spring is not powerful enough, if the timing is not perfect, or if the

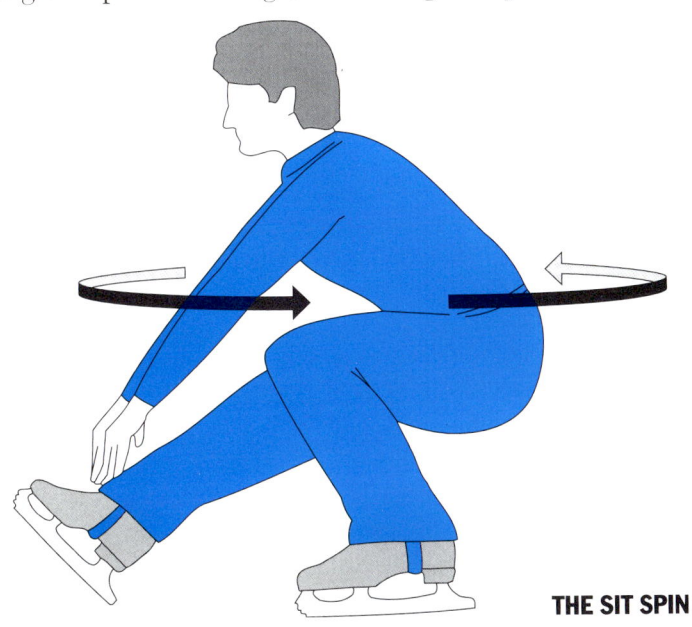

THE SIT SPIN

twist into the rotation is not smoothly executed, then a skater will enter the jump off balance or will have insufficient air time to complete the jump properly; the end result is an awkward landing or a fall. Either will cause the judges to lower the score, but a fallen skater can minimize the penalty by recovering quickly. In fact, skaters actually practice falling down and recovering. These drills also teach them how to escape serious injury in a real fall.

When learning and practicing difficult jumps, skaters take plenty of bruising falls on the ice. But most skaters minimize these by using a harness when learning tough jumps. It resembles a parachutist's harness and is attached to a long rope that is looped through a track on the rink's ceiling. The coach holds the loose end and pulls it taut should the skater falter or fall in a jump.

COMPETITORS

It is perhaps risky to generalize about people who reach the Olympic level of any sport, but many appear to share certain characteristics. A seemingly obsessive drive for perfection and an abiding love for their sport are two common traits.

It has been said that figure skaters, particularly singles and pair skaters, must dedicate more time and effort to attain championship-level in their events than competitors in any other Winter Olympic sport. It is not unusual for a medal-winning Olympic figure skater to have been bitten by the sport at about eight or nine years of age. And then, as if possessed, the aspirants persevere for up to forty hours a week, week after week, through rigorous on- and off-ice practice and training for the next ten to fifteen years. The road to an Olympic medal in skating takes dedication, self-discipline, and the utmost confidence.

For most skaters, off-ice training includes intensive classes in ballet to help teach physical expression, form, grace, balance, and poise. As with ballet, most moves in figure skating are done with the back straight, the chin proudly raised, and the arms gracefully extended from the body.

Most figure skaters in singles competition are relatively short and wiry but have powerful, well-developed legs. An average-sized male skater might be 5'6", 140 pounds; a woman, 5'2", 100 pounds. A compact stature provides more stability and balance on the ice, yet taller Olympic skaters do benefit from appearing more graceful and projecting a "good line." (That is a ballet and figure-skating term that one coach defines as "presenting a presence on the ice that's larger than life." It is an attribute that judges look for and regard highly.)

In pair skating, the man is usually taller and more muscular (about 5' 8", 155 pounds) than his singles counterpart and is also usually taller than his partner. This extra strength allows him to lift his partner more easily and to help propel her into spectacular throw jumps. They would have a much harder time achieving these feats if they were of similar size.

In ice dancing, on the other hand, the skaters are typically closer to each other in height, which enhances their appearance as a unified couple. Because overhead lifts and throw jumps are prohibited in Olympic ice dancing, there is no particular advantage to having a smaller woman as partner.

An ice-dancing couple's height and style can make the prescribed dance rhythms an advantage or a hindrance. Couples who are tall and lean can project an elegance that benefits from the tempos of a waltz, tango, or fox-trot. Those who are short and quick can give a crisp and spirited performance that is enhanced by a march, cha-cha, or quick step.

Top-caliber figure skating is very demanding, both physically and mentally, and championship levels of fitness cannot be sustained for long. In pair skating, the men usually reach their peak by their mid-20s and the women by their middle to late teens. In singles, men tend to reach their skating apex around age 25–28 and women by about 20. In ice dancing, where maturity and refinement count a bit more, couples may reach their best by their late 20s.

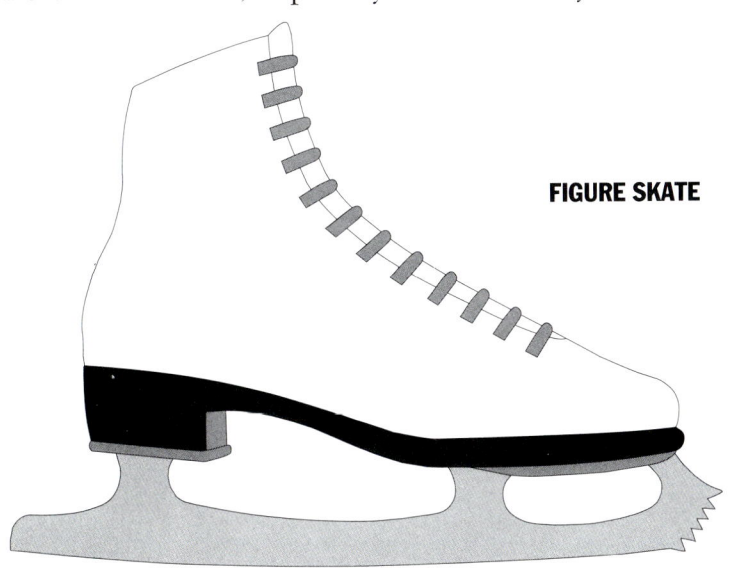

FIGURE SKATE

The jagged "toe pick" at the front end of the blade is a distinctive characteristic of the figure skate. It is useful in some types of jumps as a means of "planting" one foot at take-off, and it provides a degree of stability for the skater in a fast spin. Because jumps are not allowed in ice dancing, the toe pick is much smaller than on singles or pair skates. The bottom of a figure-skate blade has a groove running its length, giving the blade an inside and an outside edge. The blade itself is about 1/8" wide and 12" long.

EQUIPMENT

Olympic-caliber figure skates are usually custom crafted for the skater's feet and cost from $700 to $1,200 a pair. The construction emphasizes support of the foot and ankle, so the boot is made of very stiff leather with reinforcement of the arch and instep, then cushioned with a foam liner. The blades, which screw into the sole and heel, are usually made of chrome-plated, high-grade Sheffield steel, which holds a sharp edge. A pair of replacement blades costs from $300 to $500.

Costumes are also very expensive. Designed and cut by highly paid specialists, a skater's costume is carefully designed to enhance the performer's appearance and to flatter every pose. Costumes for men and women are often made of Lycra. The women's outfits, especially, are often highlighted with beading or rhinestones and sometimes feathers. Prices range from about $700 to $2,000.

HISTORY

Figure skating traces its heritage to eighteenth-century England, but it took an American named Jackson Haines to reshape a rather stuffy pastime into a dynamic sport, full of artistry, power, and technique.

In the 1860s, Haines combined his talents for dancing and skating to revolutionize figure skating. Rather than follow the staid and formal style of English skating of the time—when precise steps and repetitive patterns or "figures" were revered—Haines brought dance, music, and artistry into the rink. His balletic, fluid moves introduced a new perspective to figure skating with jumps, spins, and graceful poses. Haines, who died in 1875, is also credited with having developed the modern skate, with a blade that screws into the heel and sole of the boot.

By the turn of the century, the Swede Ulrich Salchow was attracting attention with his on-ice athleticism and exciting mastery of new and difficult maneuvers. Another Swedish champion, Gillis Grafstrom, dominated the sport throughout the 1920s and helped establish the precise, intricate patterns that evolved into the compulsories of modern competition.

The sport received its seminal shot of show biz in the form of skating sensation Sonja Henie, the Norwegian champion who won ten straight world championships (1927–36) and three Olympic gold medals (1928, 1932, and 1936). Henie then launched a very profitable professional career, which included starring roles in ten Hollywood movies as well as lavish ice shows that toured the world. She not only dared to skate like the men, with powerful jumps, but was also the first champion to wear short skirts and white boots on the ice.

Skaters soon began including double jumps in their competitive programs, and after World War II, American champion Dick Button set the standard even higher with an impressive arsenal of triple jumps and new, innovative moves.

Today, triple jumps are standard ordnance among virtually all Olympic singles and most pair skaters. In singles, most top male skaters can complete three in-air rotations in five different jumps; most top female skaters can achieve triples in four types of jumps. A few skaters are now pushing through to quadruple jumps, usually a quadruple toe loop.

Throughout the 1990s, the best Olympic figure skaters are expected to herald from the former Soviet republics, Canada, the United States, Japan, and probably China.

(See also Speedskating History, page 105.)

All great pair skaters and ice dancers project an undefinable sense of unity when skating together. This special relationship on the ice usually takes years to nurture and distinguishes good performers from truly great ones.

ICE HOCKEY • 50

Ice Hockey

Considered the world's fastest team sport, ice hockey is known for its spectacular teamwork, lightning speed, improvised plays, and temperamental flare-ups.

While skating on sharp blades and wielding long flat sticks, heavily padded players aggressively try to maneuver a puck across a sheet of ice and knock it into the opposing team's goal. Because goals are difficult to make and count only one point each, scores in this sport rarely go into the double digits.

Although hockey might at first seem difficult to follow because of its fast and unfamiliar action, the basic play is similar to two other popular sports, soccer and basketball. Two teams compete on a regulation playing area, with a goal at each end, and the objective is to attack the opposing team's goal to score points.

THE RINK

Played on a sheet of ice called the "rink," measuring 100 feet wide by 200 feet long, the game's action is contained by "the boards," a retaining wall that surrounds the rink. A red line across the center of the rink divides it in two. Marked crosswise by two blue lines, the rink is divided into thirds: two "end zones" and one "neutral zone." In each end zone, there is a goal cage and a

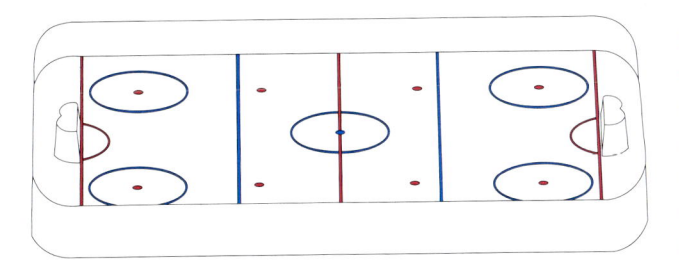

The action takes place on an inch-thick sheet of ice called the "rink"; it is about half the size of a football field and is surrounded by a retaining wall.

red goal line, which runs the width of the rink. There are also nine "face-off spots," four in each half of the rink and one in the middle.

THE TEAMS

Each team can have six players on the ice at one time—three forwards, two defensemen, and one goalie. While assigned positions are offensive or defensive, most of the players also assist in any capacity needed. In addition to the players on the ice, each team can have up to seventeen players on the bench to use as substitutes when on-ice players get tired, penalized, or hurt.

The Goalie

Unlike his five teammates on the ice, the goalie generally stays in one area of the rink. His sole job is to stop the puck from entering his team's goal cage, so he guards it closely. He rarely skates away from the small, marked-off area (called the "crease") in front of the cage. Because he must block the high-velocity puck, oftentimes with his body, he is the most heavily padded player on the team. As the only player allowed to catch and throw the puck, the goalie wears a big mitt on one hand. He also carries a broader stick than other players, and both arms are heavily padded for blocking. He's the tough, sturdy, fearless type with an intimidating presence, a keen sense of anticipation, and very fast reflexes.

Defensemen

Commanding the end zone in front of the goalie are the two defensemen, one guarding the left side, the other the right. When the puck carrier from the opposing team enters into this zone (called the "attacking zone" of the puck-carrying team and the "defensive zone" of the defending team), it is the job of the defensemen to impede the carrier's progress and break up play by checking (blocking), by deflecting any pass or shot, and, if possible, by stealing the puck. Working together as a highly skilled team, they are the last line of defense before the goalie.

Defensemen are agile yet have plenty of strength for body blocking. They also must be particularly good at skating backwards because, as the puck car-

Each team consists of six players on the ice—(A) a goalie, (B) two defensemen, and (C) three forwards.

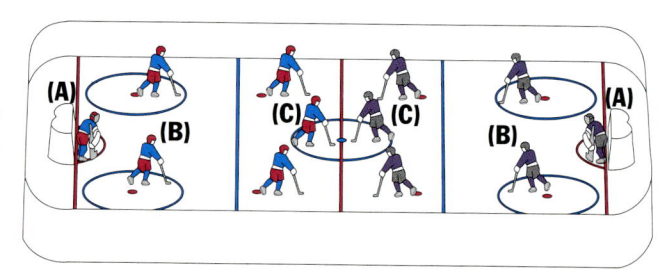

rier enters the attacking zone, a defenseman will typically position himself in front of the carrier and move with him, keeping his back to the goal. A good defenseman always tries to stay between the puck carrier and the goal, acting as a barrier and striving to thwart any attempt at scoring.

Forwards

Three players form the forward line—the center, the left wing, and the right wing. They are primarily responsible for an aggressive offense designed to carry the puck deep into their attacking zone (the opponent's defensive zone) and for attempting to shoot the puck for a goal.

The center is usually the key player on the team and the most versatile. As the player who guides the offensive action, he is strong and imposing, yet quick on his skates and able to handle the puck with force and finesse. Although a good shot-maker, he will often pass the puck with split-second timing to one of the wings, who then attempts to score the goal.

The wings, both left and right, are usually the fastest skaters and the best shooters. Working in concert with the center, they are quick thinkers who keep relentless pressure on the opposing goalie and defensemen.

THE ACTION

A game is divided into three twenty-minute "periods," which are separated by two fifteen-minute intermissions.

Play begins at center ice with a "face-off." On opposite sides of the "spot," the center from each team waits for the referee to drop the puck onto the ice. As it hits, each player immediately tries to knock it with his stick to a teammate. This procedure is repeated after each goal is scored and after certain penalties.

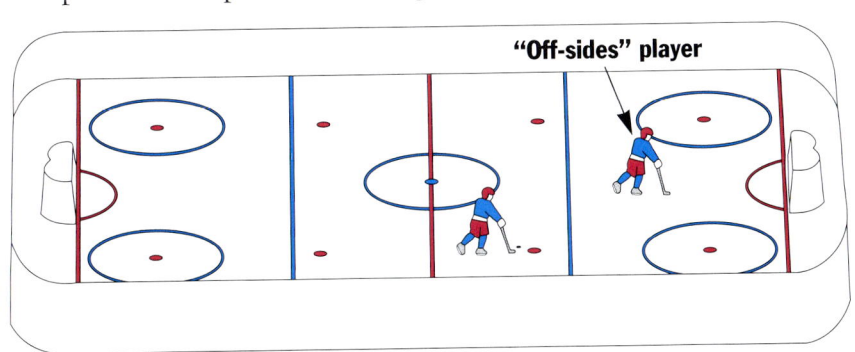

"Off-sides" player

The puck must always be carried or shot into the attacking zone before other attacking teammates may enter it. "Off-sides" is called when an offensive player crosses the blue line into the attacking zone (the opposition's end zone) ahead of the puck. The penalty is a face-off.

The team that gains possession of the puck after the face-off immediately tries to maneuver it toward the opposing team's goal. This is done by passing it from one teammate to another or by one player "stickhandling it up ice" (pushing it along the ice with his stick). Meanwhile, the defending team's players try to intercept passes or steal the puck.

As the attacking team advances the puck into the end zone, play quickens and intensifies. Upon seeing an opening, the player with the puck instantly attempts to smack the puck through for a goal. At the same time, the defending players are doing everything in their power to block the shot.

Shooting and Passing the Puck

Shots at the goal cage are made with one of two swings—the wrist shot or the slap shot.

With the wily wrist shot, the player takes a short backswing and then, without lifting the blade of the stick off the ice, snaps it forward against the puck. Because the wrist shot can be executed quickly, it is difficult for the opposing team to anticipate. A more controlled and accurate shot, it is used much more often than the slap.

The real crowd pleaser, however, is the slap shot. Hit almost like a golf swing, with a full windup and follow-through, it is the big power shot. What it loses in accuracy it gains in speed and intimidation. A well-hit puck can travel 85–100 miles per hour and is very difficult to see, much less block.

Both shots can be made so that the puck either glides along the ice (hit "flat") or flies in the air (a "flip"). The shot or pass struck flat is executed with

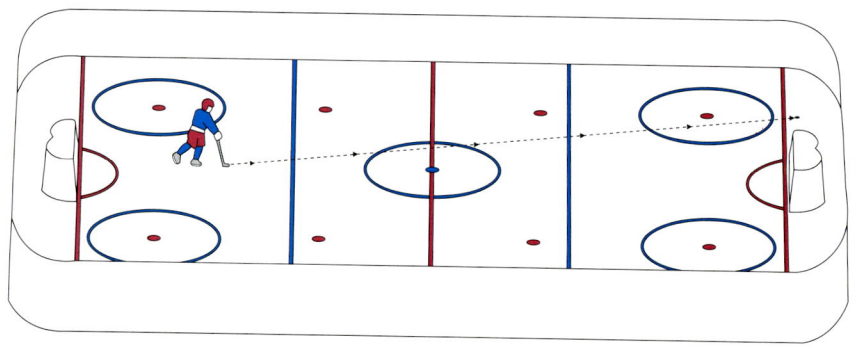

If players were allowed to slam the puck from one end of the rink to the other, not much ice hockey would get played and the sport would deteriorate into boring monotony. Therefore, if a player hits the puck from his half of the rink across the goal line of the opposing team, an "icing the puck" violation is called, play is stopped, and the puck is faced off in the offending team's end zone. While a team is playing shorthanded, however, it may ice the puck.

A player can legally deliver a forceful block, called a "body check," to an opposing player only when that player has the puck.

the blade tilted down, and the puck is hit near the heel of the blade. With the flip, the blade is tilted up and makes contact with the puck near the blade's toe. A little more wrist action is used with the flip to make the puck rise higher, but given too much "flip," the puck can soar over the boards and into the audience.

Passing the puck from one teammate to another is a very important aspect of hockey because it is the quickest way to maneuver the puck and outwit the opposition. The three basic passes are the flat pass (the puck glides along the ice), the flip pass (the puck rises off the ice), and the drop pass. In the drop pass, the player skating with the puck suddenly leaves it behind for another teammate to take immediate control of.

Checking

The "body check," the main reason for hockey's rough reputation, is simply a block, designed to knock the stuffing out of the player with the puck and give control of it to the opposing player. It is perfectly legal, so long as it is only delivered against the player with the puck.

A defensive player can legally deliver a body check only with the shoulder, hip, or torso. An effective body check will knock the puck carrier down or away from the puck, spoil the offensive play, and give the defense a good chance to steal it.

The "stick check" is another defensive move, designed to steal the puck or at least knock it away from the offensive carrier. To execute a stick check, the defensive player tries to knock the puck away from the carrier with a "poke" (a one-handed stab at the puck with his stick) or a "sweep" (sweeping his stick blade along the ice at the puck in front of the carrier).

PENALTIES

To prevent hockey from becoming a donnybrook on ice, there are many rules fortified with stiff penalties. Most are meant to discourage unnecessary roughness and injury; all are enforced by three on-ice officials—the referee and two linesmen. Just outside the rink are seven other officials: the game timekeeper, the penalty timekeeper, the official scorer, two goal judges, and two penalty bench attendants.

Basically, the rules state that a player is not allowed to hit another with his stick or even to raise his stick in a menacing, intimidating manner. The various illegal stick handlings are aptly named: "butt ending," "cross-checking," "high sticking," "spearing," and "slashing."

Players can also be penalized for body checking an offensive player who is not carrying the puck (called "interference") or for intentionally crashing into a defensive player ("charging" and "unnecessary roughness").

All these illegal acts momentarily stop the play and are punishable with a variety of penalties. Most include the temporary banishment of the offending player to the penalty bench or "box," which is a glassed-in booth beside the rink. While he is in the box, the penalized team must continue the game

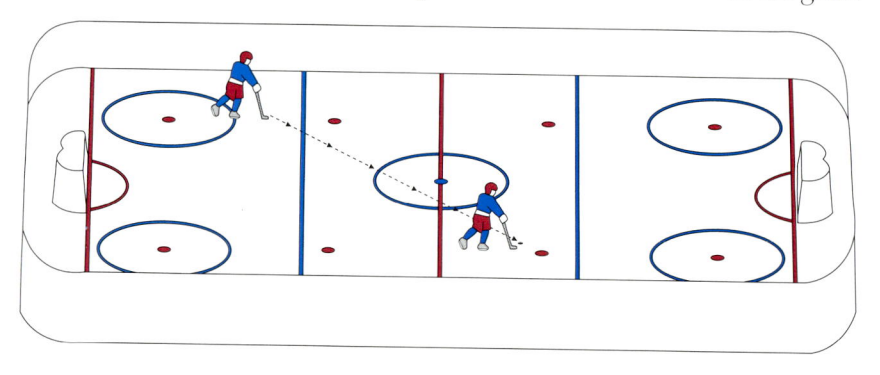

An "offside pass" is called against a player who passes the puck from within his team's end zone to a teammate on the other side of the red center line. The penalty is a face-off in the offending team's end zone.

with only five players. This is called playing "shorthanded." During this time, the opposing team outnumbers the penalized team and tries its best to score while having the advantage. This is called "power play" hockey. (Note: The rules permit no more than two players from a team to be in the penalty box at one time; if a third player is sent to the penalty box, his team can put in a substitute to maintain at least four players on the ice.)

After play has been stopped because of a penalty, it resumes with a face-off, usually at the face-off spot closest to where the violation occurred.

The basic penalty categories are:

Minor: a violation for holding or tripping an opponent or for hooking (holding him back with the blade of the stick). A player with a minor penalty must spend two minutes in the box, and his team must play shorthanded for the duration of the penalty or until a goal is scored against them.

Major: a more serious violation, usually involving illegal use of the stick. The penalty is five minutes in the box, and the team must play shorthanded for the entire five minutes. If a player receives two majors, he is ejected from the game.

Misconduct: usually given for cursing or threatening one of the officials. The penalty is ten minutes in the box, but the team can use a substitute player during that time. A player who receives two misconducts is ejected from the game.

Match: levied for deliberately trying to hurt another player. The guilty player is ejected from the game, and his team must play shorthanded for five minutes before putting in a substitute.

Penalty Shot: awarded if the puck carrier in the "attacking zone" has an unobstructed shot at the goal, but is fouled from behind as he attempts to make the shot. The fouled player is given the puck at center ice, and all other players leave the ice except for the opposing goalie. The puck carrier goes against the goalie, one on one, and is allowed a one-shot attempt on the goal. A penalty shot always provides high drama, but more than half the time the goalie blocks the shot.

Three other violations that happen frequently during a game are "offsides," "icing the puck," and "offside pass" (see illustrations, pages 53, 54, and 56).

STRATEGY

Once a team gains possession of the puck, it will advance toward the opposing team's goal with the three forwards in front and the two defensemen trailing about a zone behind; that team's goalie, of course, stays behind to guard the goal. Often, the center will skate with the puck into the attacking zone while the two wings swiftly fan out to each side in anticipation of a pass. Maneuvering the puck back and forth, the offense will try to deceive the defenders and draw them away from the goal to take a clear shot.

The best area from which to shoot is directly in front of the cage—an area called the "slot"—because the defending goalie is forced to protect the entire mouth of the cage. For this reason, defense gets roughest when the attacking puck carrier enters the slot.

During a "power play" (when one team is shorthanded because it has a player in the penalty box), the game intensifies dramatically. The team with the advantage will apply tremendous pressure to the opposing team and will attempt as many shots as possible during the penalty time. Usually, of course, it will try to pass the puck to its unguarded player for a clean shot at the goal.

Meanwhile, the team with the disadvantage will resort to defensive "penalty killing" hockey. Trying to compensate for its handicap, the team will play extra hard and ice the puck—the only time icing is legal—as frequently as possible to keep it out of its defending zone. The shorthanded team will often form a four-man "box" defense in front of its goalie to give maximum coverage to the slot area.

Hockey can be a rough game and injuries are not uncommon. Players wear thick gloves, safety helmets, and lots of protective body padding.

EQUIPMENT

Safety Gear

Hockey is a game of sudden and unexpected moves that can lead to bone-jarring impact. Accidents happen, and injuries can be serious. Therefore, all Olympic players wear protective helmets with plexiglass face shields, gloves, and plenty of body padding underneath their uniforms. There is padding to protect their shoulders, ribs and sternum, shins and elbows, and more to protect their hips, groin, and lower back. The goalie's padding is heavier than that of the other players and includes especially thick shin pads; he also wears a face guard that is attached to his helmet.

The Skate

The hockey skate is a stiff boot with a blade on the bottom that is slightly curved, or "rockered," to permit quick turns and stops. The gleaming steel blade is kept sharp to bite into the ice for the best possible traction. On the boot at the back of the ankle is a special protective strip of leather to guard the Achilles tendon from being sliced by an errant stick or skate blade.

The Stick

Hockey sticks are usually made of hardwood, but they can also be fiberglass, aluminum, or graphite. The shaft can be no longer than 58" and the blade no longer than 12 1/2" (the goalie's stick is a little broader with a slightly longer blade). The blade is often wrapped in tape to help guide the puck.

HOCKEY SKATE

The Puck

The puck, sometimes called the "biscuit," is a black disk of solid, vulcanized rubber. It measures three inches across, is one inch thick, and weighs about six ounces. The puck is frozen before a game to keep it from bouncing too much along the ice.

ICE: THE COLD, HARD FACTS

In hockey, there is good ice and bad ice; some rinks just skate and play better than others. This is usually due to the nature of the ice itself. An ideal hockey surface provides a hard, smooth sheet of ice. Hard ice, with an optimum temperature of about 19°F (-7.2°C), permits a player to get a good bite with his skate blades for quick turns, stops, and starts. Smooth ice, which is maintained by the careful grooming of an expert, allows the puck to glide fast and accurately and gives the players a predictable surface on which to skate.

The foundation of most hockey rinks is a giant slab of concrete, beneath which lies a network of refrigeration pipes to freeze the concrete and the water poured over it. To form a playing surface, a quarter-inch of water is sprayed over the concrete and then frozen. After that surface has been painted white, another quarter-inch of water is sprayed over it and frozen. Then the lines are put down using paint, strips of special paper, or cloth. After a final half-inch of water is applied and frozen, the surface is ready for play. Depending upon the facility, the entire process takes about fifteen hours and costs approximately $1,200, including the cost of water (about 10,000 gallons), paint, and electricity.

What's a Zamboni?

Most rink surfaces are groomed by an odd-looking machine with an odder name—the Zamboni. It is named for Frank Zamboni, a Californian who combined an Army Jeep, a water tank, and a cutting blade to invent the first ice resurfacing machine in 1949. The newfangled machine was popularized by the great Olympic figure-skating champion Sonja Henie, who took it on her ice show tours all over the world to insure a smooth, gleaming surface wherever she performed.

The Zamboni prepares a perfect playing surface before the hockey game and again during the two fifteen-minute intermissions. It automatically shaves the ice, gathers the shavings, and then lays down a thin layer of hot water, which quickly freezes to form a smooth, glassy surface. The operator drives the four-wheeled Zamboni around the rink in ever-tightening circles while making fine adjustments to the shaving blades and water nozzles. Performing a job that once took 1 1/2 hours, this ingenious machine can resurface an Olympic-sized rink in twelve minutes.

HISTORY

The origin of ice hockey is hazy, but most sports historians trace it back to eastern Canada during the 1860s, when British soldiers came up with a game of batting a ball on ice between two goal lines. A decade later students at Montreal's McGill University set down some basic rules. And in 1893 hockey was introduced at the U.S. college level with a match between Yale and Johns Hopkins. That same year the Canadian governor general, Lord Stanley of Preston, first offered a silver bowl to the best hockey team in Canada. A century later the Stanley Cup remains the preeminent prize among all the professional teams of the National Hockey League (NHL).

Ice hockey was included as a charter sport in the first Winter Olympics in 1924 (Chamonix). The Canadian team won, which launched its virtual monopoly of Olympic ice hockey until toppled by the Soviet Union in 1956 (Cortina d'Ampezzo). And, with a few exceptions, the Soviets have ruled ever since, including the Unified Team's victory in 1992 (Albertville). Although Olympic ice hockey is currently only a men's event, beginning in 1998 (Nagano), women's ice hockey will be introduced as an Olympic medal sport.

The U.S. team has managed to capture the glory twice by winning the gold in 1960 (Squaw Valley) and again in 1980 (Lake Placid). Because of the broad TV coverage of the matches in 1980, millions of Americans were ecstatic when the U.S. team conquered the heavily favored Soviet Union 4-3 in the semifinals and clinched the gold by beating Finland in the finals, 4-2.

In addition to the strong teams of the new Russian confederation, the United States, and Canada, the teams from Sweden, Germany, Finland, and the Czech Republic are also considered serious contenders for Olympic medals in ice hockey throughout the 1990s.

Unlike professional hockey, a fight during an Olympic match is a rarity. The penalty is severe and can include ejecting the guilty players from the game.

LUGE • 62

The Luge

Imagine lying on a simple sled, face-up and feet-forward, your head just three inches from the ice, speeding down a frozen mountainside faster than interstate traffic. This, essentially, is the sport of luge.

As one of the more dangerous of all Winter Olympic sports, the luge requires three elements for successful competition—nerve, concentration, and technique. A luger, or "slider" as the racers are often called, rides a deceptively simple-looking sled down a troughlike track of ice with maximum speed being the sole objective.

There are one-person sled races for both men and women, as well as a two-person competition. A 1992 rule change now permits the coach to choose two men, two women, or a mixed pair for the two-person event. In the singles event, each luger races down the track four times, the recorded times are totaled, and the lowest combined time wins the gold medal. In the doubles, each two-person team races twice, and the lowest combined total wins the event.

The length of the sled run for the women's and the doubles race is 10–15 percent shorter than for the men's singles. Otherwise, the same rules apply to all of the events. The primary rule in luge is "hold on to your sled." Sliders who fall off in the turns are disqualified only if they let go of their sleds.

RACING THE LUGE

The race begins on a platform at the top of the chute with the slider sitting on the sled and holding two handles attached to the start gates. When ready, the racer pulls hard on the start handles to propel the sled forward, paws the ice a couple of times with gloved hands for more momentum, then quickly "settles," or assumes the racing position (lying flat on the back, arms snugly at the sides, legs outstretched with toes pointed forward).

An electronic eye activates a time recorder at the start and finish lines, and the elapsed time is recorded in one-thousandths of a second. One run takes about fifty seconds with speeds reaching 80 miles an hour and heavy G-forces of 3–4 in the curves.

Once out of the gate, the less the slider steers, the faster the sled goes. Steering requires counterforce against the line the sled is traveling and therefore produces more friction between the steel blades and the ice. Because the luger must guide the sled for about 70 percent of the race, particularly in the curves, extra friction must be reduced by making all course corrections with a bare minimum of force and frequency. A sense of daring, quick reflexes, muscle control, and tremendous concentration are all required as the luger rockets down the run.

The racer's three greatest enemies are skidding, bumping against the sides of the track, and bouncing the sled—even slightly—into the air. All will slow the sled.

The first two problems are usually caused by oversteering. Along the bottom of a sled's two curved runners are special steel alloy blades or "steels." Part of the inside edge of each blade is sharp to grip the ice and provide traction to hold a desired course down the track. If a luger tries to apply too much steering force, the edge will lose its grip in the ice and the sled will skid sideways, losing forward momentum and time. If the sled skids too far, the luger will slam a shoulder hard into the side wall, slowing the sled down even more and requiring additional steering to regain the course.

If the sled hits a bump that causes the blades to rise off the ice, the cold air will cool the steel, also slowing down the racer. This is because friction heats the steel blades as they run across the ice, which then turns a very thin layer of the ice's surface molecules into water. That film of water, called "melt water," acts as a lubricant for the blades and makes the sled go even faster. So an experienced luger attempts to avoid bumps and to stay relaxed.

A slider with relaxed and limber muscles absorbs bumps better than one who is tense and rigid. This allows the sled to conform to the track's contours, keeping the blades in constant contact with the ice and continually generating a path of melt water. A luger who relaxes on the run is said to "gel out."

Maintaining "The Line"

Every luge track or "run" is different, so it is up to the lugers and coaches to analyze each twist, turn, and straightaway to determine the optimal path to follow for maximum speed and efficiency. That invisible, natural course is called "the line" and is what every competitor seeks. The best lugers not only find it, but also are technically skillful enough to follow it.

In the straightaways, sliders usually use what is called passive steering. If the luge is on course, the slider just stays relaxed and lets it fly down the ice with little or no course correction. But if off course or in the curves, active steering must be used to regain the line or to take the banked turns in their natural arcs and at just the right height. Otherwise, the sled will skid, bang against the wall, or lose control and possibly flip. At 70 miles an hour, contact with the ice will burn off sections of the slider's Lycra suit and can cause painful skin burns.

Although there is no steering mechanism on a luge, there are several ways to steer it. The most direct means is for a slider to press against one of the curved runners with the inside of the leg. This redirects the runner and urges the sled in the direction that the pressure is applied. For example, if the luger presses in against the right runner with the right leg, the sled will veer to the left. This type of steering gains the most immediate result, but its forcefulness also creates the most friction, resulting in the greatest decrease in speed.

Another, more subtle method is for the slider to press down with a shoulder against one of the rear sides of the sled, also redirecting the runner.

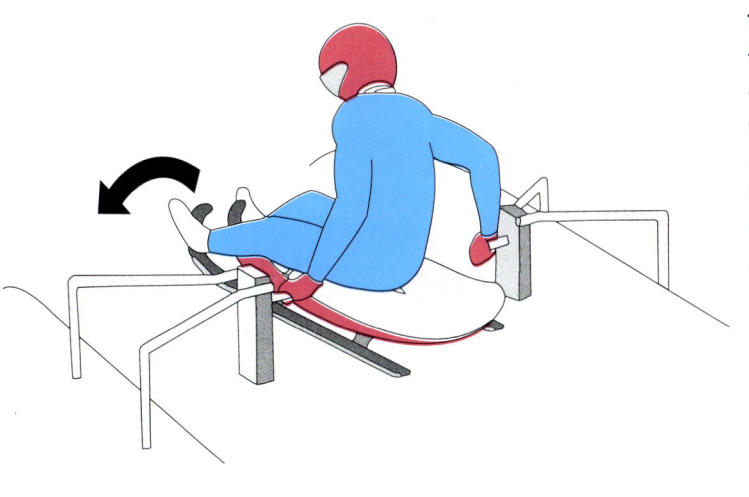

To begin the race, the luger pulls hard on the start handles to propel the sled down the ramp and into the run. Upper body strength is essential for a fast, aggressive start, which experts consider key to capturing an Olympic medal.

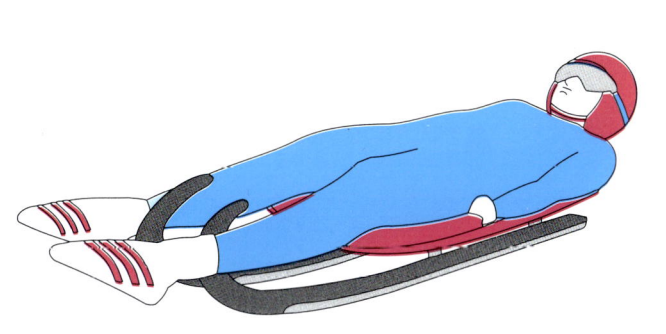

A luger races feet first, lying flat on the back, and guides the sled by pressing in on the runners with the legs to go left or right. More subtle steering can be done by pressing down with either shoulder.

Pressing the left shoulder down makes the sled turn slightly to the left and vice versa. An even more delicate maneuver is called the "head roll"; the slider simply turns the head slightly left or right, thereby applying a bit more pressure to one side or the other.

In the two-person luge, the slider on the bottom is the driver; he or she is the one who does most of the steering. The teammate on top is responsible for shifting weight in unison with the driver. The two practice long hours together to act in concert and to learn not to counteract one another's movements.

COMPETITORS

Weight, strength, and a trim physique mean a lot to a luger. Up to a point, a heavier slider will skim down the run faster because weight will help overcome wind resistance on the straightaways, where the highest speeds can be attained. Because the lighter weight luger generates less centrifugal force in the turns, however, the steels will dig into the ice with less force and produce less friction to slow the sled down.

Because body weight can affect the outcome of a race, Olympic rules permit lighter lugers to add weight by wearing special "weight vests," which have thin lead squares sewn into the liners. The lighter the luger, the more weights he or she can add to the vest—up to a maximum of 28 pounds. No extra weight can be added if the male slider weighs more than 198 pounds or the female more than 165 pounds. Most are not that big, however, because a lean body will cut through the air more efficiently, decreasing wind resistance and increasing speed. A typical male luger might be 6', 175 pounds. Female lugers average about 5'7", 145 pounds.

In summer training, a luger focuses on upper body muscle development by using weights and machines. Upper body strength is very important at the "pull start" of the race because the slider uses plenty of muscle to propel the

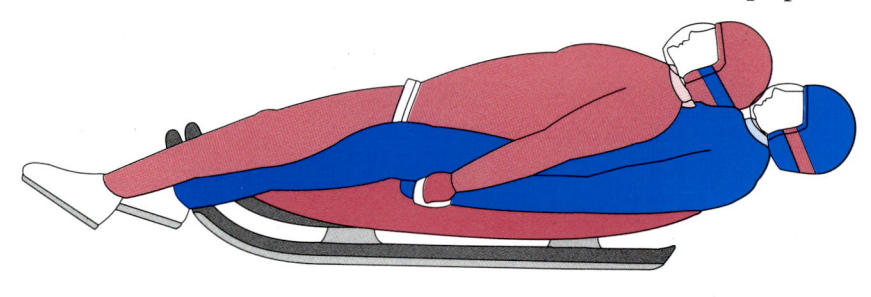

In the two-person luge, the team member on top must shift weight in unison with the driver—who is on the bottom—to help steer the sled.

sled out of the start gates. A little extra momentum at the gates can make a critical difference as the luge accelerates down the run.

During the four-month winter racing season, lugers enter the World Cup circuit for invaluable practice and competitive experience. And as the Winter Olympics approaches, most sliders visit the site for practice runs. Generally, an Olympic luger will have taken at least forty runs down that particular track before the actual Games begin.

When practicing, sliders endeavor to memorize virtually every curve and straightaway on the course so that in competition they will not need to look down the course frequently. Keeping the head back and down minimizes wind resistance. Familiarity with the track's every twist and turn also permits the racers to establish a rhythm and to visualize the run before the race as a way to deepen concentration.

EQUIPMENT

The Sled

An Olympic luge is a precision-made sled composed of technologically advanced materials. Nowadays, it is almost always handcrafted and costs upwards of $5,000 to build.

The rules stipulate that the one-person luge cannot weigh more than 51 pounds; the maximum weight for the two-person is 58 pounds. The platform upon which the luger lies is called the "pod" and is usually made of fiberglass. About 4' long and 22" wide, it is carefully fabricated to fit the luger's body contours, to be flexible for steering, and to be aerodynamic for speed.

The pod rests upon two crossbars or "bridges," which in turn are attached to the sled's twin "runners." Curved in front, the runners are made of wood, fiberglass, or composites. Along the bottom of each runner is a steel blade

The spiked fingertips of the luger's gloves are used at the critically important start. After the pull start, the spikes provide traction when the luger paws the ice several times for extra speed.

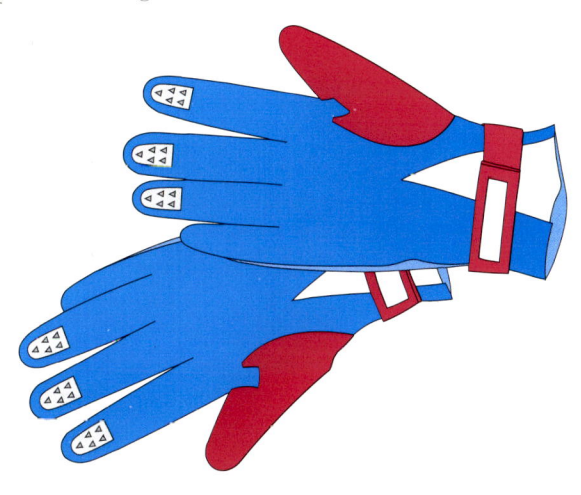

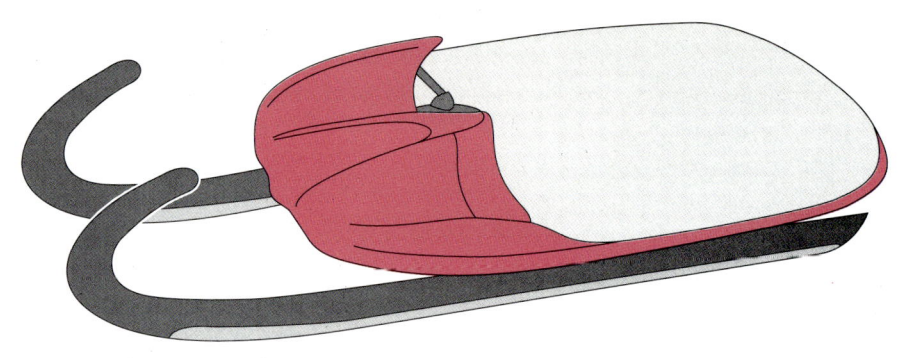

The luge, or sled, weighs about 50 pounds and can attain speeds up to 70–80 miles per hour. For Olympic competition, most are custom built of steel, fiberglass, and wood at a cost of about $5,000.

upon which the sled glides on the ice.

These blades or "steels," set eighteen inches apart and made of a special steel alloy, are the most critical components of the luge. They must be perfectly sharpened and polished and slightly turned outward so that only the inside edges touch the ice. Most importantly, they must be absolutely parallel.

Until the late 1980s, the best luges in the world were crafted by the famed Germina company in the small German town of Schmalkalden. But in recent years, the most advanced sleds are being custom made in Italy, Austria, and the U.S. as well. For those all-important steels, however, many teams still depend on a small Austrian company named Gasser.

Racing Gear

To minimize surface drag along his or her body—which can account for up to 10 percent of overall wind resistance—a slider wears a skintight, rubberized body suit and booties. All Olympic lugers must wear a Uvex helmet constructed of kevlar and fiberglass as well as a protective face shield.

Competitors also wear special gloves with small, metal spikes protruding from the fingertips. At the beginning of the race, the tiny spikes increase traction when the luger paddles a few strokes along the ice for extra momentum. A strong start can decide a closely contested race. Just one-tenth of a second gained at the start gate can culminate in a savings of three-tenths of a second at the finish line.

The Track

Because luge tracks cost millions of dollars to construct, there are fewer than twenty in the world. The long, winding trough is cradled by more than thirty miles of coiled refrigeration pipes, which circulate an ammonia-based coolant. The unit keeps the manufactured surface ice at about 22° F (-5.6° C).

Although they vary in length and configuration, luge tracks are always about 5' wide and average 1,250 meters (4,100 feet) long with about a dozen turns, including a minimum of one S-curve.

HISTORY

The word luge is French for sled. As a sport, luge can trace its heritage at least as far back as A.D. 800 to records of Vikings having made sleds with two runners. By 1480, sled races were being held in Norway. And the world's first international meet took place near the winter resort of Davos, Switzerland, in 1883.

Ever since the luge was introduced as an Olympic medal sport in 1964 (Innsbruck), the event has been dominated by the Germans and Austrians. Italian and Soviet athletes have also won many medals.

Although sliders from the United States have won medals in World Cup competitions, they have never won an Olympic medal. But the U.S. Luge Association hopes to change that as recruitment and training of its team members steadily improve, thanks in part to an excellent indoor practice run which opened in 1992 at the association's headquarters in Lake Placid, New York.

One of the main reasons for the U.S. team's lackluster luge record is cultural, according to some experts. Throughout Europe, children grow up skimming down snow-covered hills on toboggans and luges—flat on their backs, feet first. American youngsters, on the other hand, use sleds designed for the sledder to lie on his or her stomach and proceed head first, using a steering bar mounted on the front.

When an American child decides to train to become an Olympic luger (the Luge Association will accept pupils at age twelve), he or she must forget all about childhood sledding and begin learning about the luge from scratch. By contrast, a twelve-year-old child in Europe has already logged several years of luging excitement and experience.

A keen memory for a track's curves helps make a champion luger. The fewer times the head is lifted to see, the less wind resistance is created and the faster the sled goes.

SKIING • 70

Skiing

Skidding around a willowy flag pole, a lone skier sprays out a white cloud of snow. Another spins in the air like a barnstorming stunt plane, landing safely just in the nick of time. Crouching low on clattering skis, still another streaks down the icy mountainside, headed for a dangerous turn. This is Olympic skiing.

In Olympic skiing there is great variety, excitement, and drama. Some events take extra nerve to win, some take technical mastery, and some take tenacious endurance. All, however, center upon the focused determination of the skiers, each of whom has trained long and hard to perform just a hair better than the rest. That is where the excitement comes in.

BASIC EQUIPMENT

To cut down on wind resistance, skiers wear skintight, one-piece ski suits, made of smooth, stretchable material similar to Lycra. Their stiff boots are made of tough plastic and attach to the skis with special mechanisms called bindings. In a bad fall, the bindings are designed to release to help prevent ankle and leg injuries. For most events, a safety helmet is also worn.

The length and stiffness of skis can vary a lot depending upon the event and the size of the athlete. For most events, however, skis range from about 6'4" to 7'2" long (195–220 cm), are 3–4" wide, and are composed of fiberglass laminates with a wood or foam core, thin steel strips along the edges, and a smooth, polyethylene bottom.

Ski poles are used in most events to push off from the start gate (where an electronic eye activates the time clock) and to assist in maintaining balance

> Olympic skiing competition falls into three event categories:
>
> | **Alpine** | **Freestyle** | **Nordic** |
> |---|---|---|
> | Downhill | Moguls | Ski Jumping |
> | Super Giant Slalom | Aerials | Cross-Country |
> | Giant Slalom | | Nordic Combined |
> | Alpine Combined | | |
> | Slalom | | |

down the course and in making sharp turns. A pole's shaft is usually made of aluminum with a molded plastic grip on one end and a plastic or rubber "basket" on the other. The dish-shaped basket prevents the ski pole from sinking too far into the snow.

BASIC TECHNIQUES

Olympic skiing includes a very broad and exciting array of events, all of which share some fundamental principles and techniques. Two of the basic principles of skiing are following the "fall line" and maintaining control.

The steepest, shortest, and fastest path down any given slope is called the fall line. To minimize both the distance skied and the race time, competitors will usually try to follow this invisible route as closely as possible; when successful, they are said to have skied a "tight line." Because of obstacles, however, the skier usually cannot follow the shortest path exactly. Nevertheless, all maneuvers down the slope are performed with the fall line in mind.

To maintain control at fast speeds and in quick, sharp turns, the competitor must guide the skis expertly while continually keeping balanced. Proper balance comes from keeping the knees flexed and the shoulders, arms, and torso steady and square to the bottom of the slope.

Controlling the direction of the skis is usually accomplished by holding the skis parallel and close together while steering with the lower body: the hips, legs, knees, and ankles (see illustration, p. 76). The legs and knees exert the effort and side-to-side movement needed to force the skis left or right in the turns; they also absorb the jarring shocks of bumps at high speed.

To make a turn on the slope, the skier always relies on the "downhill ski." In an arcing turn to the left, for example, the right ski becomes the downhill ski. As both knees shift to the left, more weight is placed on the right ski with pressure applied to its inside edge. Conversely, for a right turn, the skier shifts the knees to the right and shifts weight onto the left ski, applying pressure to its inside edge.

In sharper, faster turns, these techniques are applied with more force and exaggeration, and "setting the edge" of the downhill ski becomes more critical. Applying pressure to the inside edge of the downhill ski provides control and keeps the ski from skidding sideways.

ALPINE SKIING

The Alpine events take place on slopes designed to test both speed and agility, but with an emphasis on one or the other. The courses that emphasize speed are long, wide, steep, and involve fewer turns. Those that accentuate turning techniques and quick footwork are shorter but studded with an array of color-coded flagpoles called gates. Competitors must ski a prescribed path around the gates, and missing one means automatic disqualification.

In Alpine skiing, the downhill and super giant slalom (called the super G) are considered the speed events, while the slalom and giant slalom are the technical events.

THE DOWNHILL

The Olympic gold medal for the downhill is considered skiing's most hallowed prize. This event presents a daunting test of speed, nerve, and physical fitness. When describing this most daring of all Alpine events, skiers often talk of high risks and of pushing the envelope. One skier who had competed and lost explained that he was "too sane to win."

On an Olympic downhill course skiers can reach 80 mph in the straightaways, or chutes. The men's course is typically 1.5 to 2 miles long with a vertical drop of 800 to 1,000 meters (2,625 to 3,281 feet). The women's course is about 1 to 1.5 miles long with a vertical drop of 500 to 700 meters

(1,641 to 2,297 feet). There are long straightaways, broad turns, fewer gates than a slalom event (about 30–35 for men and 25–30 for women), and half a dozen drop-offs that cause the skier to become airborne for 30 to 100 feet.

A contestant is permitted just one run in the finals of the competition. Depending on the course, a run usually takes from 1:45 to 2:00 minutes and is timed to 1/100th of a second.

Racing Strategy

It has been said that a downhill racer must strike a balance somewhere between madness and discipline. At such high speeds, the tiniest mistake can spell disaster. Yet an overly cautious approach will not claim the fastest time, which is all that counts in this event.

Successful racers seek to ski a tight line down the course by anticipating the quickly changing terrain. They set and hold the edge of the downhill ski in the broad turns, keep their weight forward, and assume the aerodynamic tuck, or "egg," position in the straightaways.

Tell-tale signs of a downhiller in trouble are flailing arms (loss of balance) and spraying snow in the turns (not holding the edge and skidding). Both mistakes waste time and pull the skier off the fall line and out of good position to take the next straightaway or turn properly. An open or upright position when airborne invites a loss of balance and increases wind resistance, also slowing the skier down. While in the air, the skier should assume the aerodynamic tuck position.

Surface conditions play a big role in determining racing strategy. Fresh snow favors the "glider," who excels on a smoother course. Icy conditions

The most daring of all Alpine ski events, the downhill is a spectacular challenge to the skier's mind and body. While a good recreational skier might attain speeds of 15–25 mph, an Olympic downhill racer can hit 80 mph. In the fast straightaways, the racer assumes the aerodynamic "egg" position, which maximizes speed by minimizing wind resistance.

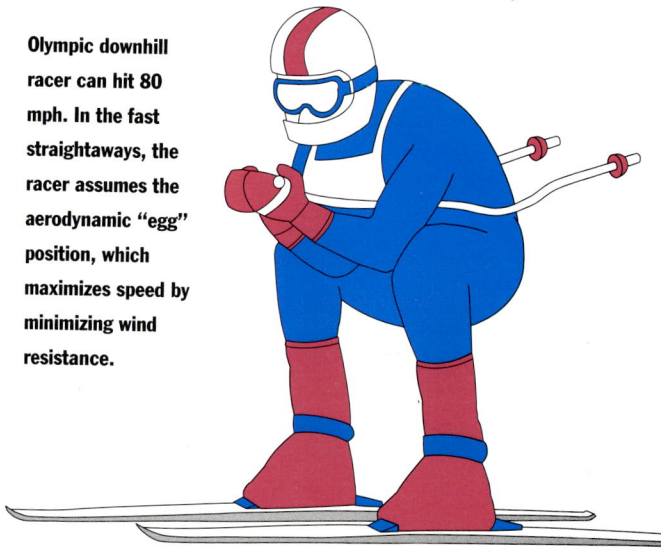

The first Winter Olympics to be televised was held in Cortina d'Ampezzo, Italy in 1956.

cater only to those skiers who are particularly good at setting their edges in the dangerous turns.

The Competitors

Although the size of downhill skiers varies, the average build is about 5'10", 180 pounds for men, and about 5'6", 140 pounds for women. These are superbly conditioned athletes whose very muscular legs, particularly the hamstrings and quadriceps, act as shock absorbers down the grueling course and provide the power to handle the turns.

In recent Olympics, the best downhillers have usually been Swiss, Austrian, or German. Although this event made its Olympic debut in 1948 (St. Moritz), a medal has been captured by an American man only once—the gold in 1984 (Sarajevo). American women have won two silver medals ('60 and '92) and two bronze ('72 and '76) in the downhill.

Equipment

The downhiller's skis are long (6'11"–7'2" or 210–220 cm; for women, 200-215 cm) to give more speed and better stability. The longer the ski, the fewer pounds will be exerted per square inch of surface space and the faster it will go.

Unlike most ski poles, the downhiller's are bent so that in the straightaway tuck position the baskets curve behind the body and do not contribute to wind resistance.

Because of this event's speed and danger, all competitors must wear crash helmets.

SUPER GIANT SLALOM (SUPER G)

The super G is a close cousin to the downhill. This event also focuses on speed with contestants reaching 60 mph. The course is somewhat shorter than the downhill, however, and there are a few more gates in order to place a little more emphasis on technical skills. There are about 35–45 gates in the men's competition and 30–40 in the women's.

Depending on the course, the super G takes about 1:15 to 1:40 minutes to run and has a vertical drop of 500–650 meters (1,641–2,133 feet) for the men's and 350–500 meters (1,148–1,641 feet) for the women's. Like the downhill, super G racers are permitted just one run in the finals.

This event challenges skiers with changing terrain, bumps, chutes, and more high-speed turns than in the downhill. Because of the need for more control, the super G skis are not quite as long as those in the downhill; they are about 6'11" (208–215 cm; for women, 200–210 cm).

Considered an exciting cross between the downhill's breakneck speed and the giant slalom's more technical demands, the super G became an Olympic medal event in 1988 (Calgary).

GIANT SLALOM

Many skiing enthusiasts claim that the giant slalom is the purest of all Alpine races because it strikes the best balance between speed and technique. Run on a slightly shorter course than the super G, there are about 35–45 gates for the men's course and 30–40 for the women's to test the skier's technical abilities, yet racers still attain speeds up to 55 mph. The vertical drop of the giant

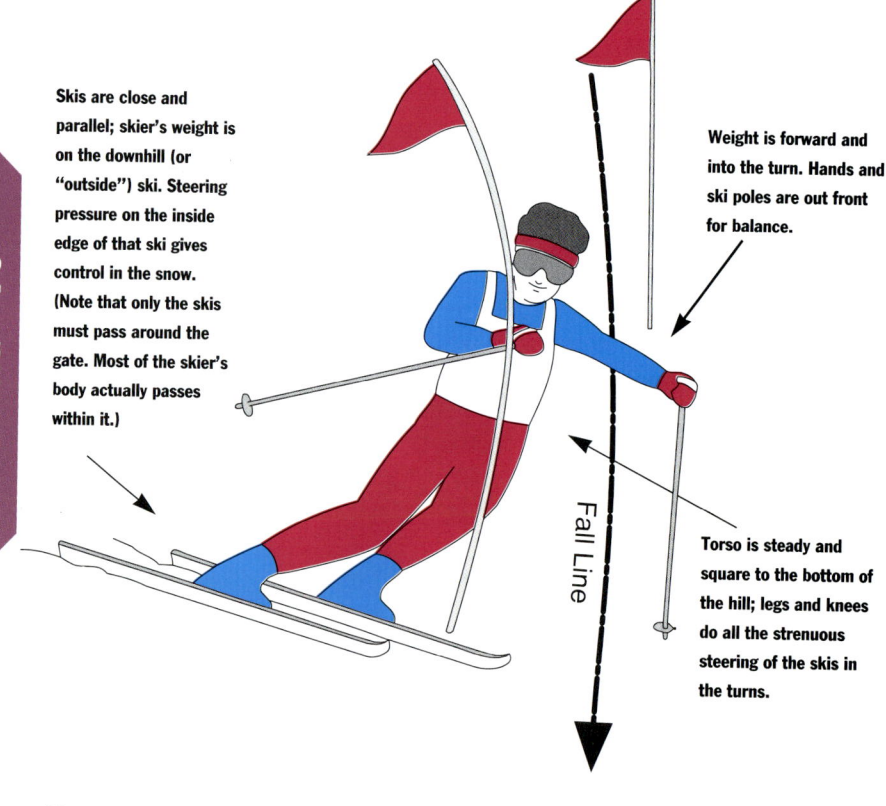

Skis are close and parallel; skier's weight is on the downhill (or "outside") ski. Steering pressure on the inside edge of that ski gives control in the snow. (Note that only the skis must pass around the gate. Most of the skier's body actually passes within it.)

Weight is forward and into the turn. Hands and ski poles are out front for balance.

Fall Line

Torso is steady and square to the bottom of the hill; legs and knees do all the strenuous steering of the skis in the turns.

The slalom racer cuts around each gate very closely for the fastest time possible down the course. Since only the skis must pass around each spring-loaded pole, the skier's body usually flattens each pole, which will pop back up. The poles are deftly deflected with the hand, forearm, or shin.

slalom course is 250–400 meters (820–1,313 feet) for men and 250–350 meters (820–1,148 feet) for women.

Unlike the downhill and super G, the giant slalom requires that each skier make two runs. The times for both are added for a combined score. Depending on the course, a good time for one run ranges from 1:05 to 1:40 minutes.

Contestants use straight ski poles in this event. And because additional gates demand more technical control, the skis are a bit shorter than for the super G—about 6'10" long (204–212 cm; for women, 195–208 cm).

Giant slalom made its Olympic debut at Oslo in 1952. In more recent Olympics, the event has been won mostly by skiers from Italy, Switzerland, and Austria. Throughout its prestigious history, the giant slalom has never relinquished a gold, silver, or bronze medal to an American man. American women, on the other hand, have captured six medals.

SLALOM

Long considered Alpine skiing's litmus test for agility, quick reflexes, and technical skills, the slalom pits the skier against a rapid succession of gates placed strategically down the course. A series of short, quick turns requires the slalom racer to cut around a pole—alternately colored blue or red—every second or less (see illustration, opposite page). Although the descent rate rarely exceeds 25 mph, the action is constant and feverish.

A run in this action-packed event takes about 45–50 seconds to complete, depending on the course, and includes 55–75 gates in the men's run and 45–60 in the women's. In the finals, each skier does a run on two different courses, and the times are combined for a total score. Sometimes the two courses are set up adjacently on the same slope, sometimes on two different slopes. The vertical drop for a slalom course ranges from 180 to 220 meters (591–722 feet) for men and 130–180 meters (427–591 feet) for women.

Olympic slalom competitors are in top condition with the average build for men about 5'8", 160 pounds. There are, however, some successful slalom skiers who are bigger, about 6'1", 200 pounds. Women are generally about 5'5", 125 pounds.

The Italians, Germans, Austrians, Americans, and French have usually done well in both men's and women's slalom in recent Olympics.

Course Strategy

At the Olympic level of slalom competition, technical skill and exceptional athletic ability are not enough; all of the athletes have these strengths. It is here that superior concentration, willpower, and—some say—intuition can play a critical role in winning or losing the event.

Above all the athletes must remain focused, yet be able to rely on years of training and well-honed reflexes to guide them down the course. Or, as one racer put it, the best strategic approach in the slalom is to "be brainless."

Whatever the approach, the racer must not be distracted by danger or possible risks, but must set the ski edges quickly and decisively and take the turns early to be in optimal position for the next gate.

Equipment

Because of the emphasis on quicker turns and more control, slalom skis are about 6'6" (195–205 cm; for women, 185–204 cm), the shortest of all skis for Alpine events.

The gates, or flagpoles, are made of thin, flexible plastic with a hinged, spring-loaded base so that they pop back up when flattened by the racer (see illustration, p. 76). These gates are hazardous, not so much because of the chipped teeth, split lips, and skin welts they can cause if a skier does not deflect them skillfully, but because a pole slap can break the skier's concentration and cause a split-second loss of time. That is critical in an event where half a second can mean the difference between an Olympic gold medal and no medal at all.

The gates are blocked aside by the slalom skier's hand, forearm, or shin. Hard strips of plastic and foam padding are affixed to the ski suit at these and other contact points for protection.

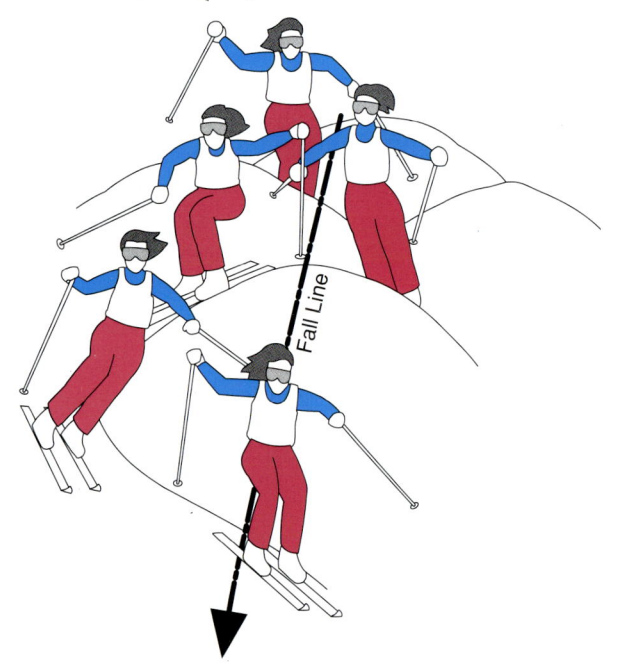

A mogul skier keeps both eyes directed down the course in order to read the field. Head, shoulders, hips, and hands point downhill and stay relatively motionless for balance while legs and knees act as shock absorbers and direct the skis. Quick, precise turns are made by exerting pressure on the inside edges of the skis to bite the snow.

ALPINE COMBINED

This demanding two-day event includes one downhill run the first day and a slalom run on two different courses the next. The three times are added together for a total score. It is interesting to note that the medal winners in this event are usually good at one type of skiing and excellent at the other rather than being equally accomplished at both.

In recent Olympics, the Italians, Swiss, and Austrians have done well in the Alpine combined, an event that was reinstated in 1988 after a forty-year absence. (For history of Alpine skiing, see page 95.)

FREESTYLE SKIING

Moguls and aerials, the two Olympic "Freestyle" events, were fashioned in the 1960s and 1970s by rambunctious young skiers intent upon catapulting beyond the bounds of traditional skiing. Freestyle skiing remains the province of flashy twists and turns, of airborne acrobatics, and of astonishing stunts.

MOGULS

When competing in this event, the skier resembles a very agile pinball ricocheting down the mogul course. Encountering about seventy-five moguls in less than thirty seconds, the competitor must rapidly make precise moves from one snow mound to the next. Mogul comes from the German/Austrian term meaning "small hills."

An Olympic mogul course slopes about 28 degrees and measures approximately 230 meters long by 30 meters wide (755' x 98'). It is covered with hard-packed snow mounds 2–4 feet high. The larger moguls are placed at one-third and again at two-thirds of the way down the bumpy course for the

THE TWISTER

skiers to use as ramps from which to jump for airborne maneuvers.

The object of mogul skiing is to negotiate the course in minimum time, and, despite the numerous moguls, to maintain good form and balance. At each of the two "ramp" moguls, the skier leaps into the air to execute a stunt-like maneuver, then continues skiing the moguls. The event presents a stiff challenge to the skier's athletic ability, technical competence, versatility, and concentration.

Acrobatics

The three most common acrobatic maneuvers done off the two jumps are

THE DAFFY

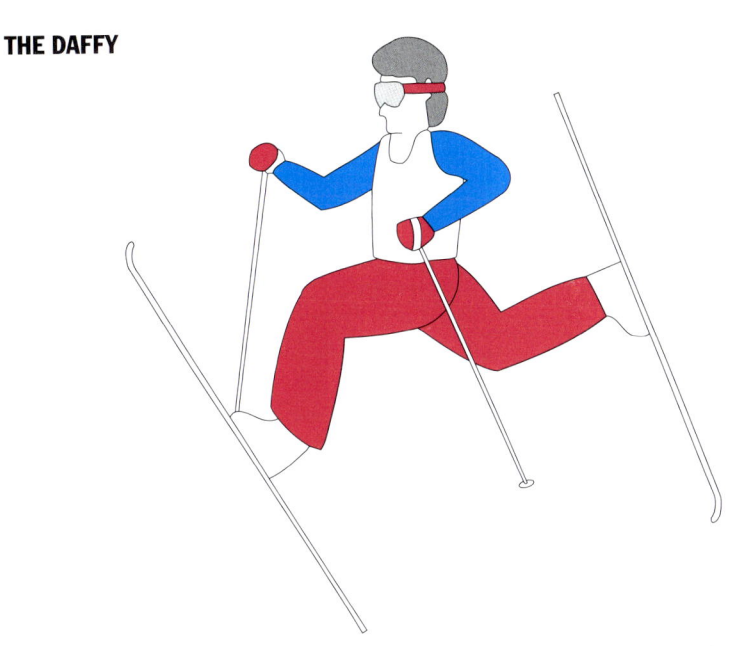

the "twister," the "daffy," (see illustrations) and the "spread eagle" (or "spread"). To score extra points, many competitors attempt to execute two to three maneuvers during one jump. Somersaults and other "inverted" maneuvers are not permitted in moguls competition.

One of the more difficult mogul jump maneuvers is the "helicopter." For this, the airborne skier rotates one complete revolution before landing (see illustration, page 82). Perfect timing is essential for a smooth, controlled landing.

Scoring

In the finals, each competitor is permitted one run down the course and is assessed by seven judges. The total score for each skier is calculated by a formula with three criteria:

Turns (technique and form): 50 percent of the total score. This rating is based upon how well the skier navigates the moguls. As the skier rapidly glances from one bump to the next while going down the course, the head and torso should be steady and the skis together and parallel. The quick, rhythmic movement is very similar to slalom racing. Judges assess penalties for falls and loss of control.

Jumps: 25 percent of the total score. For each of the two jumps, judges consider the degree of difficulty of the acrobatics and how well they are performed.

Speed: 25 percent of the total score. Men usually complete the course in

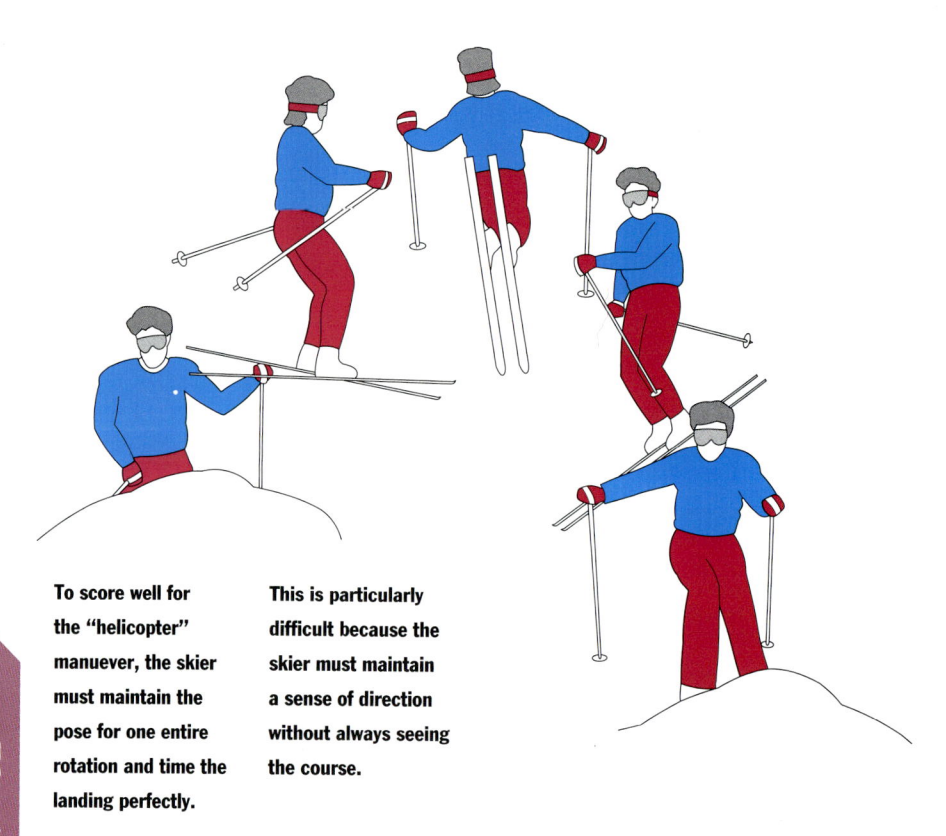

To score well for the "helicopter" manuever, the skier must maintain the pose for one entire rotation and time the landing perfectly.

This is particularly difficult because the skier must maintain a sense of direction without always seeing the course.

25–30 seconds, women in 30–35 seconds.

Strategy

A successful mogul skier analyzes a course to determine the best route, which is a compromise between the "fall line"—an invisible line that is the fastest, shortest, and steepest route down—and the arrangement of moguls, or snow bumps. Each racer decides on a path down the course that permits quick and rhythmic skiing while also demonstrating proficiency of skills.

With the multiple aspects of scoring, the competitor not only must ski quickly down the course for a fast time, but also must demonstrate virtuosity, style, and technical proficiency to score well in the jumps and turns categories.

Difficult, high-scoring jump maneuvers require good height in the air, which eats up time on the clock. Likewise, while well-executed deflective turns from one mogul to the next look stylish and impressive to the judges and the crowd, they also require valuable time. Therefore the skier must constantly balance speed against showy maneuvers and the need to demonstrate technical proficiency.

While establishing a good, fast, rhythmic pattern through the mogul field, the competitor must also prepare for the two jumps. The airborne maneuvers must be completed cleanly and with very good balance because more moguls confront him the instant he lands.

Competitors and Equipment

Unlike the loose, informal training of pioneering mogul skiers in the late 1960s and throughout the 1970s, training today is stringent, disciplined, and year-round. In addition to logging plenty of practice hours on the mogul course, competitors also put in lots of off-course hours building up leg strength, working on gymnastics skills, and increasing reaction speeds.

Mogul skiers use ski poles to help them push off for a quick start at the top of the course and to assist them in making precise turns as they glance from one mogul to the next.

The men use skis measuring about 6'4" (195 cm), women about 5'10" (180 cm). Protective helmets are not worn in this event.

AERIALS

Because of the daring stunts and showmanship involved, aerials is one of the most thrilling Olympic skiing events to watch. Leaving the ramp at 35 mph, the skier is hurled as much as three stories high to perform spectacular airborne acrobatics.

The course for the Olympic aerials event consists of a hillside about 240 feet long, which the competitor skis down to build speed for the ramp called the "kicker." Each skier chooses one of three different-sized kickers from which to jump—one for single somersaults, one for doubles, and one for triples. Although somersaults are illegal in moguls competition, they are mandatory in aerials.

The triples ramp shoots the skier approximately 35 feet in the air, almost straight up. While airborne, each competitor performs a set of acrobatic maneuvers in front of a seven-member panel of judges before landing on a slope 50 feet down the hill. In the finals for both the men's and women's divisions, each competitor performs two jumps, and the scores are combined for a final score.

Scoring

The jumps are evaluated through a scoring formula with three criteria:

Air: 20 percent of total score. This rating is based upon how well the skier takes off from the ramp and whether sufficient height and distance are attained to execute the acrobatics properly. Judges pay particular attention to a strong, bold take-off.

Form: 50 percent of the total score. Judges look favorably on airborne acrobatics that are executed with style and precise movement. Stability in the air and economy of motion are valued. The degree of difficulty of each maneuver is also factored into the score (for example, a good double somersault scores more points than a good single).

Landing: 30 percent of the total score. The judges look for a safe, stable, and controlled landing. The impact of the landing should be absorbed by the skier's flexed knees and lower body. Good balance, precision, and gracefulness are assessed highly.

Acrobatics

At the Olympic level of competition, most aerial maneuvers involve somersaults with exciting and innovative variations. Similar to diving competitions, the somersault positions seen most often in aerials are the "layout" (also called the "lay") and the "tuck" (see illustrations). The layout is a bit more difficult to execute than the tuck and therefore provides slightly higher points.

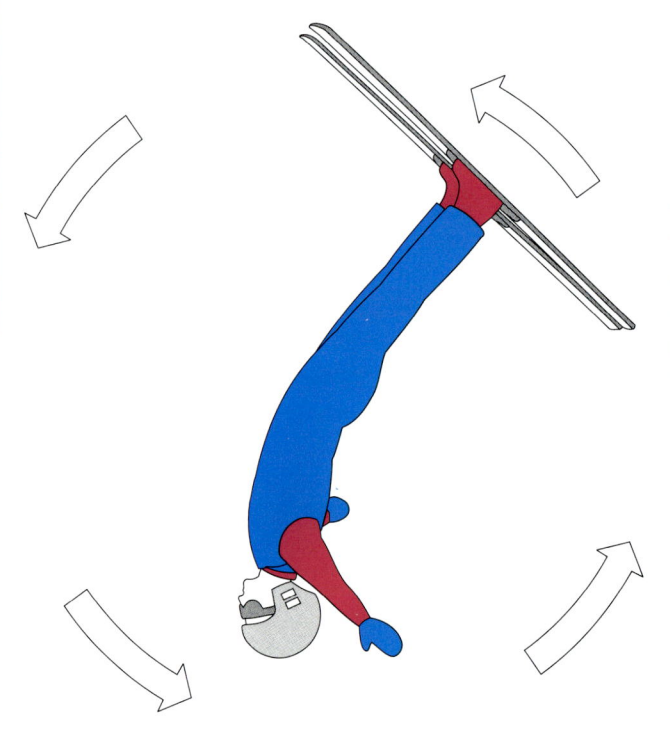

The "layout" position in a backwards somersault is considered a more difficult maneuver than the "tuck." Arms must remain outstretched and skis parallel throughout the entire somersault.

> For every Olympic Games a torch is kindled at the Temple of Hera in Olympia, Greece. It is then transported to the host country where a relay team brings it to the main stadium to ignite the ceremonial flame, which burns until the closing ceremony when it is extinguished.

Somersaults are done backwards.

Another popular movement that is usually executed in conjunction with a somersault is called a "twist," in which the skier makes one revolution on the axis running from head-to-toe. One somersault with a twist is called a "full."

With combined maneuvers, the terminology can become rather confusing. For example, if the TV commentator announces a "back lay-tuck-lay," for example, then the skier has executed a triple backwards somersault—the first and third done in the layout position and the middle somersault done in the tuck position. A "back full-double-full" jump means the skier has performed two backwards somersaults—the first with a single twist and the second with a double twist. There are dozens of dazzling combinations to watch for, including the very difficult "quadruple twisting triple somersault."

Competitors and Equipment

Because of the inherent dangers of the sport, aerialists always wear protective helmets and train with a bias for safety. Ski poles are not used. Training regimens include many hours of gymnastics as well as acrobatics on a tram-

The "tuck" is a familiar somersault position in the aerials event. Judges value precision and good form.

poline. During the warm, off-season, practice jumps are made into a swimming pool.

HISTORY OF FREESTYLE

Freestyle's colorful past has its origins in the United States where, during the free-spirited 1960s, many young skiers felt the urge to break with conventional styles of skiing in order to have more fun on the slopes and to invent more expressive, less restrictive variations of the sport.

Early freestyle skiing was loosely classified as "Hot Dog Skiing" because the skiers were stereotyped as sharing the unconventional attitudes of the legendary California surfers who were famous for their daring stunts while riding huge waves. The cold-weather hot doggers tried skiing the bumpiest terrains while introducing acrobatic stunts to the slopes.

The first freestyle skiing competitions were held in New England in the late sixties and early seventies, and, gradually, more rules and criteria were applied as enthusiasts sought broader acceptance. The sport divided into three events—moguls, aerials, and ballet—and in 1980 all three were first included on the World Cup ski circuit.

Freestyle's struggle for legitimacy gained ground when moguls became an Olympic medal sport for the first time in 1992 (Albertville) and when aerials was likewise adopted for 1994 (Lillehammer). The third freestyle skiing event, called ballet, is performed in World Cup competition but has not been accepted as an Olympic medal event. While some consider the nature of this event to be too subjective for fair judging, proponents hope it will be adopted in time for the 1998 Winter Olympics in Nagano, Japan.

Throughout the nineties, Olympic mogul skiers from the U.S., France, and Canada are expected to excel in both the men's and women's divisions. In men's aerials, the U.S., France, and Canada should do well. In women's aerials, the best skiers are expected to come from Switzerland, Sweden, and the U.S.

Tests indicate that jumpers who use the newer V ski position in flight achieve up to 60 percent greater aerodynamic efficiency than those who use the parallel ski position.

NORDIC SKIING

Nordic skiing includes two categories of events that could not be more different from one another—ski jumping and cross-country skiing.

SKI JUMPING

In the most magical of Winter Olympic events, the ski jumper zooms down a precipitous ramp at nearly 60 mph, launches into silent, soaring flight, and then, far below, lands with the touch of a snowflake. For the spectator, ski jumping provides breathless suspense and wonderment; and for the accomplished jumper, a pure, Zen-like high.

The premise behind jumping is straightforward: the individual jumper skis down a tall, icy ramp, shoots off the end of it, and attempts to glide in the air as far down the hill as possible. There are two such events in Olympic competition. The shorter of the two is called the "normal hill," with good jumps of about 90 meters, or 295 feet; the other is the "large hill," with good jumps of about 120 meters, or 394 feet. There are no women's events in Olympic ski jumping.

In both events, competitors make three jumps. The first jump is for practice; the second two count. These last two distances are added together and, according to a formula, converted into points scored. This score, combined with the judges' evaluation of the jumper's style or form in flight and when landing, comprise the final score. Distance and style each counts 50 percent of the final score.

Five judges evaluate each jump, and the highest and lowest scores for each jumper are discarded. This helps eliminate bias or misperception that a judge might have about any given jump. To measure distance traveled in the air accurately, each jump is recorded on a video system that incorporates a calibrated scale to show the exact touch-down point. Total distance is measured from take-off to touch-down, with the touch-down point being established as midway between where the two skis land.

Olympic ski jumping also includes a team event, which is held only on the large hill. Each team has four members. In the finals, there are two rounds, and each team member jumps once per round. The three best jumps per team are counted in each round, and the team amassing the most points wins the gold medal.

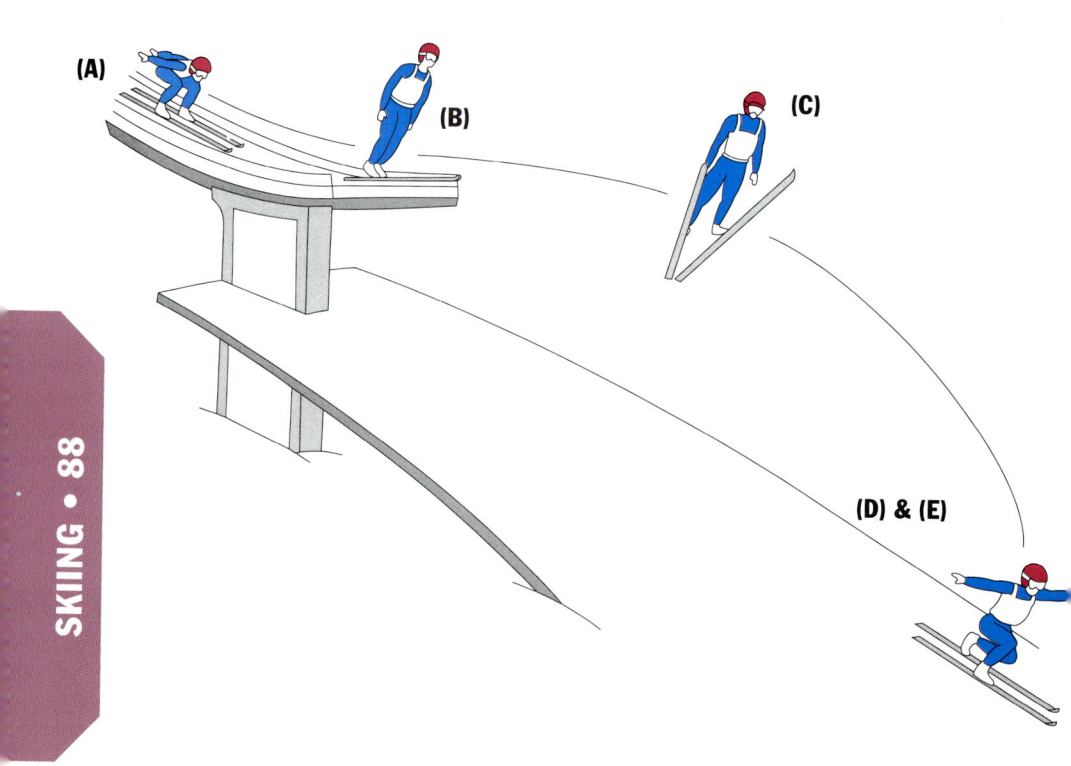

SKIING • 88

A ski jump consists of (A) the in-run or ramp, (B) the take-off, (C) the flight path, (D) the landing, and (E) the out-run. There is a red line across the landing area called the "K" point, which indicates to the airborne skier where the slope of the hill begins to flatten out into the out-run. Skiers whose flight distances exceed the K point receive extra points on their scores, but the more jarring landings on the flatter out-run often cost them points on style. For the normal hill, K is about 90 meters (295') from the take-off point. For the large hill, it is about 120 meters (394').

Depending on the hill, the in-run measures 83-90 meters long.

Although television makes it appear that a ski jumper is very high in the air, in reality the flight trajectory of the jump is roughly parallel to the slope, and the athlete is never higher than about fifteen feet from the ground.

The Jump

A ski jump consists of five phases:

The In-Run: At the top of a ramp twenty-six stories high, the competitors wait for their turns to jump. When ready a jumper eases to the edge of the ramp, then lunges down the icy slide. Maximum speed is attained by keeping the skis together and parallel and by crouching in the "egg" position to minimize wind resistance.

The Take-Off: At the last possible moment before leaving the ramp, the jumper, who has now accelerated to about 55 mph, leaps forward on his skis. Strong thigh muscles and perfect timing are essential. The purpose of this leap is twofold: to increase forward speed and to establish flight position quickly.

The Flight: Now airborne, the jumper leans his body out over his skis, which should be positioned in the newly popular V formation for added distance (as opposed to the outmoded parallel formation). The position of his body and skis enables the jumper to soar in the air for about the length of a football field before landing. In assessing the jumper's style during flight, the judges look for control, precision, and symmetry of body and skis.

The Landing: Just before landing, the skier stretches his arms out to slow his descent and prepare for a balanced touch-down. He must land in the classic "telemark" position—arms outstretched (the hands cannot touch the ground), knees flexed, skis together and parallel with one ski projecting ahead of the other. Again, judges look for control and balance as they score for style.

The Out-run: On this flat plain, the jumper needs only to ski to a stop while remaining poised, balanced, and in control.

Competitors

Despite the surprisingly low injury rate of ski jumping, it is still viewed as one of the most dangerous of all winter sports. Unquestionably, some very nasty falls have occurred, but jumpers insist that the sport is quite safe if practiced by experienced athletes under favorable conditions—not when the wind is gusty and unpredictable or when visibility is low.

The perfect physique for a jumper embodies the basic characteristics of a kite—lightweight, with enough surface area to catch the air. Also, powerful thighs are needed for the important thrust at take-off. Olympic jumpers are

A Olympic ski jumper usually remains airborne for about four seconds. Because of the extreme concentration required, some jumpers claim that they have no recollection of being in flight while others feel that they have been in the air for minutes

usually around 5'10" and 132 pounds.

Low body weight can make a big difference. One U.S. expert estimates that an extra kilogram of body weight (2.2 lbs.) can shorten a jump by two meters (6'8"). For this reason, some jumpers have been known to fast for a couple of days before a competition; a few have even induced vomiting just prior to a jump.

To train to become a ski jumper, the athlete begins by jumping from very small ramps, gradually building up competence, confidence, and distance. The in-run surface is narrow and, during the season, made of snow that has been hard-packed by machine to ensure predictable consistency. But during the warm off-season when the majority of practice jumps are made, the in-run is surfaced with smooth porcelain, which is constantly watered to keep it slick; the jumpers land on a long, padded sheet of plastic. It takes several years of dedicated training and practice to attain Olympic-caliber skills. Top Olympic contenders make about eight hundred practice jumps a year—up to fifteen a day in the off-season but no more than about six a day before an important competition.

Equipment

The skis used for jumping are monsters (up to 8'9" long and 4 1/2" wide) in order to function better as wind foils for maximum gliding and distance. But the position of the skis in flight is even more important. The recently developed V position, where the leading tips of the skis are wide apart and the trailing tails are together, provides substantially more distance than the traditional parallel position.

Using the revolutionary V, a good jumper can attain as much as forty more feet on the normal hill and upwards of seventy additional feet on the large hill. Since its inception in the late 1980s, the V has proven so much more effective that the lengths of most in-runs have been shortened because jumpers were beginning to overshoot the sloped landing areas, causing them to slam down on the flat out-runs. That difference in impact has been compared to jumping off a chair versus a fifteen-foot-high roof.

History

Ski jumping originated in Norway during the 1840s, but it was not until 1862 that it was organized as a competitive sport. Included in the first Winter Olympics in 1924, the sport was dominated by Norway during the early years of competition. Over the past two decades, however, Finland, Austria, and Germany have captured the lion's share of Olympic medals for both the normal and large hills. An American has won only one medal—a bronze in 1924 (Chamonix).

CROSS-COUNTRY SKIING

Cross-country skiing is considered to be the most physically demanding of all Winter Olympic events. Not only a grueling test of endurance, this sport also requires superior technical skills and tactics.

Both the men's and women's events are divided into two categories, those skied in the traditional or "classic" style and those skied "freestyle."

In the classic style (see illustration below), the competitor keeps the skis parallel and moves forward in long, gliding strides, pushing with ski poles. (The long, rhythmic strokes of classic cross-country skiing are simulated in

The traditional "classic" stride of a cross-country skier is smooth and efficient.

Special substances on the bottom of the skis—called kick wax and glide wax—allow

the racer alternately to glide across the snow and to grip it for secure push-offs.

Olympic cross-country events:

Men	Women
Combined Pursuit	Combined Pursuit
10K (6.2 miles) Classic	5K (3.1 mile) Classic
15K (9.3 miles) Freestyle	10K Freestyle
30K (18.6 miles) Classic	15K Classic
50K (31 miles) Freestyle	30K Freestyle
4 x 10K Relay	4 x 5K Relay

the popular Nordic-ski workout machines.) The skis gain traction in the snow because of an ingenious substance called "kick wax." Applied along 12–14" of the bottom of each ski just beneath the foot, this wax adheres to the snow when all of the skier's weight is applied. The rest of the ski is coated with "glide wax," which reduces friction to help the ski slide along the snow. A good Olympic skier can cover a kilometer (.62 miles) in about two minutes and forty-five seconds using the classic style.

In freestyle events, virtually everyone uses the "skating" style of skiing (see illustration below), which employs the same push-and-glide motion as roller skating or ice skating. Permitted for the first time in Olympic competition in 1988, the skating technique enables the skier to race faster than the classic style. A good cross-country skier using this style can cover a kilometer in about two minutes and thirty seconds. Only glide wax is needed for these skis.

Carefully prepared, the cross-country courses are configured as loops measuring from 5 to 16.6 kilometers long, depending on the race. Each course presents varying contours to challenge the skiers' uphill, downhill,

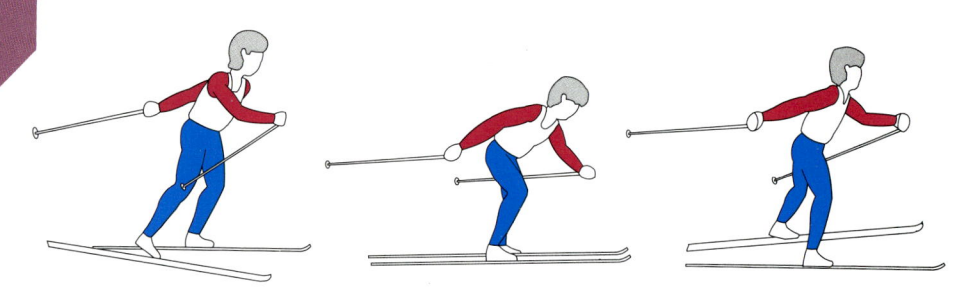

Faster than the "classic" style of cross-country skiing, the skating technique of skiing employs the same angular push-and-glide strokes as roller-skating and ice skating. Its use is permitted only in "freestyle" cross-country events.

and flat-terrain skills. In the 50K event, for example, skiers race a little more than three times around a 16.6K loop, taking about two hours and averaging around 15 mph. The number of hills and gradients for each course must conform to international skiing specifications, and special power tillers work the snow on the course to the desired texture and firmness.

The Combined Pursuit is a two-day event. On the first day, skiers, beginning at 30-second intervals, race a 10K classic (5K classic for women). The skier with the best time wins the gold medal for his or her event. The next day, the athletes ski a 15K freestyle race (10K for women). The competitors, however, begin according to how they finished the previous day. A racer who finished two minutes behind the winner of the 10K race, for example, starts the 15K race two minutes after the first skier begins. The skiers who cross the finish line first, second, and third for the second race win the gold, silver, and bronze medals for the combined pursuit. Therefore, the skiers who win medals in the first race could win two Olympic medals in the combined pursuit. Of course, it is more difficult for those who did not place well on the first day to do well in the second day's competition because of the time handicap imposed upon them.

The 4 x 10K relay for men and the 4 x 5K relay for women are team events, with four skiers per team. In this competition, each skier races one of four 10K loops (5K for women). The first two loops must be raced in the classic style, the last two freestyle. In the relay event all of the teams start together, and upon finishing a loop, the racer must tag the next teammate who then continues the race. The team with the fastest time wins the event.

Racing Strategy

The 5-, 10-, and 15-kilometer events are considered sprints, so the skiers attempt to race at full speed for the entire distance. In the longer 30- and 50-kilometer events, the skiers begin the race at a somewhat slower pace to conserve energy. They drink rehydrations—energy drinks—at "feed stations," and strategically increase speed and effort as the race progresses.

Passing can be tricky, especially on hills, so, unless they are particularly strong hill skiers, racers usually attempt to pass competitors on flat terrain. In classic races, a skier who is being overtaken must move to one side to allow room to pass. To signal an intention to pass, the approaching skier calls out "track," and the person in front must yield or risk disqualification.

Competitors

Because cross-country racing demands long, sweeping strides, top male racers are relatively tall, averaging about 5'11", 167 pounds. In recent years, some of the best men have been taller—around 6'2", 175 pounds. Women are about 5'7", 129 pounds. The competitors are lean like long-distance runners but usually have stronger shoulders and arms from working their ski poles.

Training relentlessly, cross-country skiers practice at least 30 hours a week. In the off-season, they bicycle or skate great distances on roller skis, which are short cross-country skis mounted on rubber wheels at the front and back.

Equipment

Cross-country skis are slightly shorter, lighter, more flexible, and narrower (about 2 1/4" wide) than alpine skis. Like alpine skis, they are made of fiberglass with a wood or foam core and a polyethylene veneer on the bottom. The skis used in the classic style are shaped with a more pronounced curve at the front tip and have a groove along the bottom that runs the length of the skis. This groove helps the classic skier glide in a straight line.

As a general rule, the ski for a classic-style race is about 4" (10 cm) longer than the athlete is tall. For freestyle events, the ski's length and athlete's height are about equal.

Classic and freestyle cross-country boots are both made of nylon and plastic, but their general designs differ somewhat. While each attaches to the ski only at the toe of the boot, the freestyle boot has a high-top design, giving the skier the extra ankle support needed for the angular skiing strokes. Because classic skiing is more linear in movement, ankle support is not needed. The classic boot, therefore, has a low top and is more flexible, resembling a track shoe. Cross-country boots usually cost between $200 and $275 a pair.

NORDIC COMBINED

In some circles, it is said that the individual winner of this two-day event is truly the *meister* (master) of Nordic sports because the combined includes both Nordic disciplines, ski jumping and cross-country skiing. There are individual and team competitions for men; there is no women's event.

Individual

On the first day of the individual competition, each skier must make three jumps from the normal hill. The first is a practice jump; only the second two are scored. On the second day, all competitors ski a 15K freestyle cross-country race. Each skier's starting position is determined by how well he did in the jumping event. To establish these positions, the total distance jumped by each athlete is converted into a points system, which is then converted into time: Nine points equals one minute. If a skier finishes the jumping segment

At the opening ceremony of each Olympic Games, an athlete from the host country recites the official oath: "In the name of all competitors I promise that we will take part in these Olympic Games, respecting and abiding by the rules which govern them, in the true spirit of sportsmanship for the glory of sport and the honor of our teams."

twenty-seven points behind the leader, he begins the cross-country race three minutes behind the leader. This is called a "Gunderson start." The first skier to cross the finish line of the race is the winner of the entire event.

Team

In this two-day event, there are three skiers per team. The first day is ski jumping from the normal hill, with each team member taking three jumps. (As in the individual, only the second two jumps are counted. Each person's worst jump is not counted.) The next day is the 3 x 10K relay event with each team member skiing a 10K freestyle cross-country race. As in the individual Nordic combined, the relay begins with a Gunderson start, and the first three teams across the finish line win medals for this two-day event.

Training

Both of the Nordic-combined events present major challenges to competitors because ski jumping and cross-country skiing demand opposing skills and muscle development. Cross-country skiing requires endurance, upper-body strength, and long, lean leg muscles. Ski jumping, on the other hand, favors a lean upper body with more heavily muscled thighs for explosive take-offs. Therefore, it takes a very carefully balanced training regimen to hone both sets of skills for the Nordic combined.

HISTORY OF SKIING

Ancient rock drawings in Scandinavia indicate skiing's utilitarian origins at least as far back as 5000 B.C. There is similar evidence in Siberia and Central Asia that crude skis were fashioned by prehistoric people for hunting and transport during the deep snows of winter. The oldest known ski was found in a peat bog in Sweden and dated to about 2500 B.C.

As a sport, however, skiing's history spans a mere two hundred years and claims Norway as its birthplace. Cross-country skiing was enjoyed there as a sport by the seventeenth century and was firmly established throughout the country by the mid 1800s. By the 1860s, ski jumping had been added to

In the Alpine speed events, skiers must have very strong legs to act as shock absorbers and provide enough power to handle the turns.

Norway's winter sport competitions. From the late nineteenth century, waves of Norwegian emigrants spread their beloved sports to other European countries as well as to America.

The Nordic (cross-country) ski techniques, which were developed for primarily flat and open terrain, were not very effective on the steep Alpine slopes of central Europe. So, during the nineteenth century, a new approach evolved—Alpine-style skiing, which employed shorter, thinner skis and emphasized quicker, more agile movements for turning. Benchmark books on Nordic and Alpine techniques were published during this early era and helped spread interest even further.

Although the Swiss Alps had been popular with summer travelers for some time, these awesome mountains did not entice many winter visitors until the latter half of the nineteenth century. Hardy hikers and climbers were first attracted, followed by trekkers on the newly introduced skis. Skiers, or "plank hoppers," began showing up at the Swiss resort of Davos in the 1880s, arousing curious looks and smirks from other guests—mostly British—who were accustomed to ice skates and toboggans. In 1890, ski jumping made its debut as a novelty on the slopes of nearby St. Moritz. In fact, it was members of the British leisure class who provided the early impetus and enthusiasm for winter sports at Swiss resorts and who were responsible for organizing many of the first competitions. British athletes dominated Alpine events until the early 1920s when formidable competition rose out of Switzerland, Norway, and France and brought an end to the British reign.

Improved bindings and periodic improvements in technique continued to attract more enthusiasts to skiing over the next several years. But the sport's next quantum leap did not occur until about 1930 when a young Swiss engineer named Gerhard Muller, using rope and motorcycle parts, is said to have invented the first drag line for skiers in Davos. Suddenly, the sport's popularity took off. Instead of enduring a morning's climb up a steep slope for a quick ski down, skiers could now be towed up the hill by a motorized line in ten minutes or less. This development proved revolutionary to skiing and was the forerunner of T-bars, chair lifts, gondolas, and cable cars.

In an unusual twist, the Nazi movement served to stimulate skiing's popularity in the U.S. Many Europeans, escaping German occupation and persecution, fled to America in the late thirties and forties and brought their contagious love of skiing with them.

By then, although skiing was still a little-known sport, America was already the home of Idaho's Sun Valley, the first resort ever built specifically for skiing. Quickly following was a long procession of other now-famous resorts such as Vail, Keystone, Copper, and Jackson Hole.

SPEEDSKATING • 98

Speedskating

Approaching the speed of a Thoroughbred racehorse, an Olympic speedskater is a stunning blend of power and grace. Using the strong, rhythmic strokes produced by years of relentless and dedicated practice, speedskating is the fastest a human being can travel on a flat surface without mechanical aid.

Men's and women's speedskating is divided into two classes of competitive events, those performed on the "long," or "metric," track and those on the "short" track. Long-track speedskating has been included in the Winter Olympics since the Games' inception in 1924, while short track is an exciting newcomer, having been an Olympic medal event only since 1992.

LONG TRACK

When most people think of speedskating, they think of long-track events. These are the traditional speedskating events characterized by long, graceful glides and sweeping arm motions. Competitors skate around an oval, 400-meter track (437 yards, or about the size of a standard track-and-field track).

In the men's division, the events are: 500 meters, 1,000 meters, 1,500 meters, 5,000 meters, and 10,000 meters (6.2 miles, or 25 times around the track). The first two are considered sprints, the last two endurance races. The 1,500 is a grueling cross between sprinting and endurance racing.

For women the long-track events are: 500 meters, 1,000 meters, 1,500 meters, 3,000 meters, and 5,000 meters (3.1 miles).

In all long-track events, two skaters race at a time. Their times are recorded, and after all of the competitors have raced, the skaters with the three

Top Speeds

Olympic swimmer	5 mph
Sculler	11 mph
Sprinter	23 mph
Speedskater	35 mph
Racehorse	40 mph

fastest times win the gold, silver, and bronze medals for the event.

Each lane on the long track is about fifteen feet wide, and because the inside lane covers a shorter distance than the outside lane, adjustments must be made to even the distance raced. Therefore, midway down the back straightaway of each lap, the two skaters must switch lanes, where they continue to skate until the next "crossover."

At the starting line, the racers take an odd-looking stance (see illustration). It is practical, however, because the position approximates the very beginning of a stroke. So when the starter's gun fires, the racers simply execute what they are already poised to do. There is no wasted time or motion.

To attain racing speed quickly, the skater accelerates for the first few yards by taking short, choppy strokes and swinging both arms. A quick start is especially critical in the sprints, where races can be won by a couple of hundredths of a second, or about half the length of a skate.

After the initial dash, the racer switches to the powerful, rhythmic style of speedskating that generates additional acceleration and speed. With head bent forward and torso parallel to the ice, the skater gains momentum by pushing forcefully off the back skate and gliding on the leading one. In cadence with the legs, the racer swings the arms back and forth to transfer maximum force onto the lead skate at each stroke.

The classic arm swings are not only useful for building speed in the sprints, but also help maintain speed and control in the longer races. In the 1,500 meter, for example, a speedskater usually swings with both arms for the first 200 meters and then uses only the right arm for the rest of the race. The left arm (or inside arm, since skaters race counterclockwise) rests on the skater's back.

In the endurance races, the skaters begin by stroking with both arms, but once they hit their stride, they put both arms on their backs to relax, conserve energy, and glide most efficiently. On the turns, they pump with the outside arm for power and balance. And in the last three or four laps, the skaters resort to continual one-arm strokes to compensate for tiring leg muscles and to attempt to maintain speed.

Although the straightaways are the most obvious place to gain speed, racers also generate extra momentum in the turns by using the "whip" effect. The skater comes into a curve on the outside of the lane, then gradually tightens the arc toward the inside, coming out of the turn with newfound velocity.

Everything about a speedskater's racing technique is designed to transform energy efficiently into forward motion and to minimize drag. The forward lean of both head and body cuts down wind resistance as well as lowers the center of gravity, which improves balance. Repeatedly driving the leading blade along the ice at the precisely correct angle minimizes friction, allowing for the most effective performance possible.

To get maximum speed and distance with each stroke, skaters must have flawless technique, no matter how tired they become. This consistency is achieved only after years of practice until the motion becomes second nature and can be executed without error, lap after lap.

In the sprint events, skaters maintain maximum speed throughout the race. But in the longer distances, skaters must pace themselves in the early laps, conserving energy so as not to burn out before the final phase of the

The unique stance of the speedskater at the starting line looks like a stop-action photo taken during a race. The position closely approximates the beginning of a stroke. When the start gun fires, the racer simply completes the stroke with no wasted time or motion.

race when they will need that last "kick," which could make the difference between winning and losing.

Since long-track events involve minimal interaction between racers, the skater pays little attention to the competitor in the other lane. Instead, each races against the clock, and, along with a track-side coach, keeps meticulous account of lap times, calculating to the second how fast each lap should be in order to remain in contention for a medal.

SHORT TRACK

Introduced into Olympic medal competition in 1992, short-track speedskating events gained instant popularity. Very different from events of the long track, short-track races are held on a compact, 111-meter (121-yard) track, that can fit on an indoor hockey rink. Another big difference is that four to six skaters compete on the track at a time—sometimes called "pack" skating. And skaters do not race against the clock; in the finals, the first three across the finish line win medals.

In both the men's and women's divisions, the short-track events are the same: 500 meters and 1,000 meters. In addition, there is also a 5,000-meter

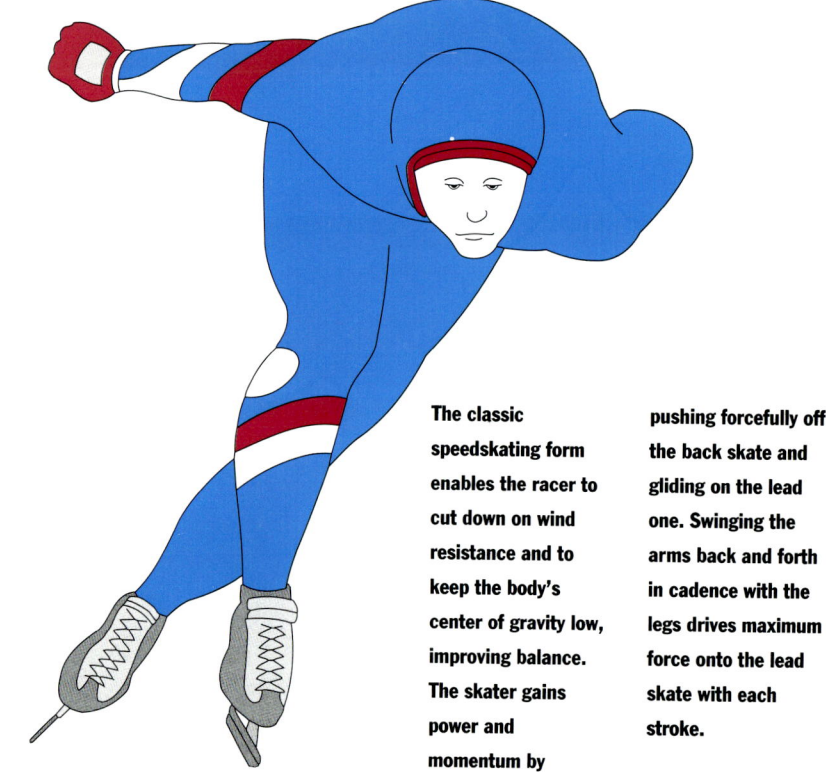

The classic speedskating form enables the racer to cut down on wind resistance and to keep the body's center of gravity low, improving balance. The skater gains power and momentum by pushing forcefully off the back skate and gliding on the lead one. Swinging the arms back and forth in cadence with the legs drives maximum force onto the lead skate with each stroke.

In 1980, U.S. speedskater Eric Heiden became the first man in Olympic history to win all five speedskating events. Not only did he capture the gold in each race, but each victory also set a new Olympic record.

relay for men and a 3,000-meter relay for women.

Fans relish the compressed action on the small track as the pack of skaters, blades clattering on the ice, race around the rink at a frenzied pace. When rounding the turns, they lean in deeply against centrifugal force, skimming their fingers along the ice to steady themselves and to fend off spills.

Although intentional contact is illegal, there are many high-speed spin-outs and trip-ups, which send hapless skaters skidding across the ice and into the padded walls. Because the leader is less likely to get jostled or tripped, gaining the lead in these events can be particularly advantageous. The lead skater, however, does not benefit from "drafting" (closely following an opponent who blocks the wind).

In the relay events, four skaters (one from each of four competing teams) race around the rink. After racing, the skater "tags" an awaiting teammate by skating up from behind and literally pushing the next racer into action. Unlike track-and-field relays, no baton is passed from one teammate to the next.

COMPETITORS

The stereotype of a long-track speedskater is a solitary individual, obsessed by the challenge of the sport. While a variety of individuals participate in speedskating, all are drawn to its rigors, precision, and competitiveness. They come tall and short, but an average male speedskater is about 5'11", 170 pounds, an average female about 5'7", 130 pounds.

Short-track skaters are usually smaller, the men about 5'9", 160 pounds, the women about 5'5", 125 pounds. They have very quick reflexes and excellent balance and are exceptionally good at drafting, passing, breakaways, dodging other racers, and sprinting.

What all speedskaters have in common are tremendously powerful thighs that provide the necessary power to propel them around the track. A recent long-track male champion had a 32" waist and 27" thighs. Another could do 30 deep-knee bends with 360 pounds of weight across his shoulders.

Training is tough and usually lasts four to six hours a day. A weekly regimen often includes running (both sprints and long distance), lots of cycling, weight lifting, and of course plenty of practice on the ice. In the off-season, many skaters train with in-line roller skates. Some also use a slide board, which is a piece of slick formica on which the skater, wearing socks, can simulate speedskating strokes.

The design of the long-track speedskate is very different from the hockey or figure skate. The shoe has a low top for more comfort and flexibility in long races. Its 16–18" blade is nearly 50 percent longer than a hockey skate blade, distributing the skater's weight over a longer edge and improving the ability to glide. The short-track blade is 14–16" long.

EQUIPMENT

The Skate

The most obvious difference between the speed skate and other ice skates is the length of the blade. At 16–18", a long-track blade is nearly 50 percent longer than other skating blades; it gives the speedskater added stability and the ability to glide longer distances. The blades for long-track skates are virtually straight. The short-track blades, which are 14–16" long, have an almost imperceptible curve, allowing them to take the tighter turns better.

Unlike the stiff, high-top boots used in hockey and figure skating, the long-track speedskate shoe is more supple, coming to just below the ankle. Although the athlete loses extra ankle support, there is more flexibility and comfort, an advantage when skating longer distances. The short-track shoe is stiffer and higher, providing more support to the ankle on the smaller track.

The ideal ice temperature for speedskating is about 27°F (-2.8°C). If the ice gets much warmer, it becomes too slow and soft for gliding. If it gets colder, the ice can become brittle, making it difficult to gain a sure grip with the blades.

The Uniform

The speedskater's racing suit, or skin, also plays that all-important function of cutting down on wind resistance. Made of Lycra, the brightly colored suits are skintight, permitting air to slip across the skater with a minimum of drag. Long-track skaters wear hoods; short-track skaters wear helmets.

HISTORY

At its primitive beginnings, probably in the Netherlands, ice skating amounted to a bone being tied to the bottom of the footwear, making it easier to traverse a frozen lake or river. There are several allusions to skating in old Norse sagas, and an Icelandic poet once sang that "Ull, god of winter, runs on bones of animals over the ice."

By the thirteenth century, blades were being made of wood. And by about 1500, iron blades were being affixed to the bottoms of wooden shoes. From Holland, site of the first recorded speedskating competition, recreational ice skating spread quickly to Germany, France, Austria, and England.

By the mid-nineteenth century, ice skating had become a very popular pastime in Europe, and by the turn of the century, it was the favorite winter sport of the fashionable set in Switzerland. In America a skating club was established in 1849, in Philadelphia, employing the long, frozen stretches of the Schuylkill River; soon, the sport was adopted in New York and Washington, D.C. In 1885 the first international race was held in Hamburg, followed four years later by the first World Championship, held in Amsterdam.

Many of history's prominent figures were skating enthusiasts, including the German poet Goethe, Marie Antoinette, William Wordsworth, Napoleon Bonaparte (who, while a student, nearly drowned while skating), Queen Victoria (whose skate blades curved up artfully in the shape of a swan's neck and head), and Henry David Thoreau (who skated on Walden Pond).

At the inaugural Winter Olympics in 1924 (Chamonix), the men's 500-meter speedskating competition had the distinction of being the first event to be completed. The first Winter Olympic gold medal went to an American named Charles Jewtraw who won the race in forty-four seconds (compared to about thirty-six seconds today).

Women's speedskating was not included until the 1960 Olympics (Squaw Valley), where the Soviet and German skaters won all four gold medals.

To help build powerful thigh muscles, speedskaters do plenty of bicycling. Some training regimens call for two hours of cycling at 80 percent of maximum pulse rate.

BIBLIOGRAPHY

Bass, Howard. *Skating Elegance on Ice*. London: Marshall Cavendish, 1980.

Bauer, Erwin A. *The Cross-Country Skier's Bible*. New York: Doubleday & Company, 1977.

Brady, Michael. *The Complete Ski Cross Country*. New York: The Dial Press, 1982.

Coote, James. *A Picture History of the Olympics*. New York: The Macmillan Company, 1972.

Flower, Raymond. *The History of Skiing and Other Winter Sports*. New York: Methuen, 1977.

Gamma, Karl. *The Handbook of Skiing*. New York: Alfred A. Knopf, 1992.

Gillette, Ned and John Dostal. *Cross-Country Skiing*. Seattle: The Mountaineers, 1988.

Petkevich, John Misha. *The Skater's Handbook*. New York: Charles Scribner's Sons, 1984

———. *Figure Skating Championship Techniques*, New York: Sports Illustrated Winner's Circle Books, 1989.

Petrick, Tim. *Sports Illustrated Skiing*. New York: Harper & Row, 1985.

Readhead, Monty. *Ice Dancing*. London: Pelham Books, 1968.

Shero, Fred, and Andre Beraulieu. *Hockey for the Coach, the Player and the Fan*. New York: Simon and Schuster, 1979.

Wallechinsky, David. *The Complete Book of the Olympics*. Boston: Little Brown & Company, 1991.

PHOTO CREDITS

front cover	Craig Blankenhorn
p. 6	Craig Blankenhorn
p. 8	Bettmann Archives
p. 9	Allsport
p. 10	Craig Blankenhorn
p. 12	Craig Blankenhorn
p. 19	Craig Blankenhorn
p. 20	Craig Blankenhorn
p. 29	Allsport/Bob Martin
p. 30	Allsport/Rick Stewart
p. 49	Allsport/Vandystadt
p. 50	Allsport/Vandystadt
p. 61	Allsport/Rick Stewart
p. 62	Craig Blankenhorn
p. 69	Allsport/Pascal Rondeau
p. 70	Allsport/Vandystadt
p. 73	Allsport/Nathan Bilow
p. 79	Allsport/Vandystadt
p. 87	Allsport/Vandystadt
p. 96	Allsport/Vandystadt
p. 98	Craig Blankenhorn
p. 105	Allsport/Mike Powell
back cover	Craig Blankenhorn

Index

Biathlon
    Anschutz rifle, 16
    freestyle, skiing, 18
    penalty loop, 14
Bobsled
    brakeman, 21-24, 27
    D-ring, 23
    Kreisel, 21
    labyrinth, 21
    pilot, 21-25, 27
    pushbar, 23
    pushman, 21-23, 27
    runners, 25, 27
    slider, 23
Boitano, Brian, 8
Button, Dick, 8, 44, 48
Colledge, Cecelia, 43, 45
Coroebus of Elis, 6
Coubertin, Pierre de, 7, 32
Eagan, Eddie, 26
Figure skating
    Axel, 38-41
    camel spin, 34, 43
    concentration, 10
    death spiral, 34
    drape, 37
    flip, 42
    flying camel, 43-45
    freestyle program, 31
    layback, 44-45
    long program, 31, 33
    loop, 42
    Lutz, 40-41
    pairs, 33, 35-36, 46, 49
    press lift, 34
    pulls, 34
    Salchow, 40-42
    short program, 31, 33
    singles, 31, 46, 49
    spiral, 34
    sit spin, 45
    star lift, 32
    tabletop lift, 32
    technical program, 31
    toe loop, 42
    toe pick, 47
    visual imagery, 32
Grafstrom, Gillis, 48
Haas, Christl, 8
Haines, Jackson, 45, 48
Hamilton, Scott, 8
Heiden, Eric, 103
Henie, Sonja, 48
Ice Dancing
    compulsory dance, 36, 38
    dance rhythms, 47
    free dance, 36, 39
    original dance, 36, 38
Ice Hockey
    biscuit, 60
    boards, 51
    body check, 55
    center, 53
    checking, 55
    crease, 52
    defensemen, 52-53, 57
    drop pass, 55
    end zone, 51
    face-off, 53-54
    flat pass, 55
    flip pass, 55
    forwards, 53-53
    goalie, 52, 59
    hockey rink, 51
    major, penalty, 57
    match, penalty, 57
    minor, penalty, 57
    misconduct, penalty, 57
    National Hockey League, 61
    offside pass, 57
    offsides, 53, 57
    penalty shot, 57

period, 53,
power play, 58
puck, 51-52
slap shot, 54
slot, 58
wings, 53, 57
wrist shot, 54
Zamboni, 60

Louis, Spiridon, 7

Luge
    Germina, 68
    Gasser, 68
    head roll, 66
    melt water, 64
    passive steering, 64
    pod, 67
    slider, 63
    steels, 64, 68

Lutz, Alois, 41
Muller, Gerhard, 97
Olympia, 6
Olympic creed, 37
Olympic flag, 6
Olympic flame, 10
Olympic logo, 6
Olympic motto, 14
Olympic oath, 95
Olympics, Summer, 7, 26
Orser, Brian, 8
Paulsen, Axel, 41
Preston, Lord Stanley of, 61
Rittberger, Werner, 42
Salchow, Ulrich, 42, 48

Skiing (Aerials)
    full, 85
    kicker, 83
    layout position, 84
    tuck position, 84-85
    twist, 85

Skiing (Alpine)
    Alpine combined, 72, 79
    downhill, 72-73, 76-77, 79
    downhill ski, 72, 74, 76
    evolution of technique, 95
    fall line, 72, 74
    gates, 75-78
    giant slalom, 72, 77
    slalom, 72, 77

super giant slalom, 72-73, 75-77

Skiing (Moguls)
    daffy, 81
    fall line, 82
    helicopter, 81-82
    hot-dog skiing, 86
    twister, 80-81

Skiing (Nordic)
    combined pursuit, 93
    cross-country, 91-95
    glide wax, 92
    Gunderson start, 94-95
    kick wax, 92
    Nordic combined, 94-95
    ski jumping (see ski jumping below)

Ski jumping
    concentration, 9
    egg position, 74
    in-run, 88-89
    K point, 88
    large hill, 87
    normal hill, 87
    out-run, 88-89
    take-off, 88-89
    telemark position, 89
    V position, 86, 91

Speedskating
    concentration, 9
    crossover, 100
    drafting, 103
    long track, 99-100
    pack skating, 102
    short track, 99, 102
    whip effect, 101

Stenmark, Ingemar, 8
Theodosius, 6
Witt, Katarina, 35
Zeus, 6, 10, 11

ABOUT THE AUTHOR

Dan Bartges began his career in 1972 as the editorial writer and cartoonist for the *Alexandria Gazette* and later became a freelance writer and photographer for the *Washington Post, Baltimore News-American, New York Post,* and others. He is now vice-president of The Martin Agency, a leading advertising and marketing firm.

His research for this book included interviews with U.S. Olympic staff, coaches, athletes, and judges, as well as visits to the Winter Olympic training facilities in Colorado Springs, Co., and Lake Placid, N.Y., where he tried both the luge and bobsled runs.

A graduate of Hampden-Sydney College and the University of Richmond, Bartges now resides in the historic Fan District of Richmond, Va., with his wife, Kelley, a public defender in juvenile court.

ACKNOWLEDGMENTS

Many thanks to the Olympic coaches, judges, staff members, and athletes for their valuable assistance with this book. I am particularly grateful to Dennis Agee, Alan Ashley, Chuck Berghorn, Bonnie Jean Carr, Janet Champion, Jeff Chumas, Jack Colter, Hugh Cooke, Deborah Engen Clouse, Matt Erickson, David Farrar, Bill Fauver, Dmitry Feld, Carol Fox, Alan Johnson, Tom Kelly, Joey Kilburn, John LaFevre, Joe Lamb, Betty Law, Katie Marquard, Kristin Matta, Paul Nicholas, Bob Paul, Matt Roy, Mark Rudolph, Darryl Seibel, Bill Spencer, Jack Vivian, Fred Zimny, the writers of *Sports Illustrated*, and especially my wife, Kelley.

"By the time the ceremonies had come to an end a typical February Adirondack blizzard raged across the stadium. The thousands assembled there lookt [sic] like snow-white ghosts in the eerie half-light. Darkness closed in as the flag came down."

—*Official Report, III Olympic Winter Games* (Lake Placid, 1932)